PINEAPPLE

Edible

Series Editor: Andrew F. Smith

EDIBLE is a revolutionary new series of books dedicated to food and drink that explores the rich history of cuisine. Each book reveals the global history and culture of one type of food or beverage.

Already published

Apple Erika Janik *Beef* Lorna Piatti-Farnell *Bread* William Rubel *Cake* Nicola Humble *Caviar* Nichola Fletcher *Champagne* Becky Sue Epstein *Cheese* Andrew Dalby *Chocolate* Sarah Moss and Alexander Badenoch *Cocktails* Joseph M. Carlin *Curry* Colleen Taylor Sen *Dates* Nawal Nasrallah *Game* Paula Young Lee *Gin* Lesley Jacobs Solmonson *Hamburger* Andrew F. Smith *Herbs* Gary Allen *Hot Dog* Bruce Kraig *Ice Cream* Laura B. Weiss *Lemon* Toby Sonneman *Lobster* Elisabeth Townsend *Milk* Hannah Velten *Mushroom* Cynthia D. Bertelsen *Offal* Nina Edwards *Olive* Fabrizia Lanza *Oranges* Clarissa Hyman *Pancake* Ken Albala *Pie* Janet Clarkson *Pineapple* Kaori O'Connor *Pizza* Carol Helstosky *Pork* Katharine M. Rogers *Potato* Andrew F. Smith *Rum* Richard Foss *Salmon* Nicolaas Mink *Sandwich* Bee Wilson *Soup* Janet Clarkson *Spices* Fred Czarra *Tea* Helen Saberi *Whiskey* Kevin R. Kosar *Wine* Marc Millon

Pineapple

A Global History

Kaori O'Connor

REAKTION BOOKS

For Phil Gusack

Published by Reaktion Books Ltd
33 Great Sutton Street
London EC1V 0DX, UK
www.reaktionbooks.co.uk

First published 2013

Printed and bound in China
by Toppan Printing Co. Ltd.

A catalogue record for this book is available from the British Library

ISBN 978 1 78023 179 2

Contents

Introduction:
Origins and Discovery

During his second voyage to the New World, Christopher Columbus came ashore on 4 November 1493 on the newly sighted Caribbean island he had just named Santa Maria de Guadeloupe, and promptly 'discovered' the pineapple (*Ananas comosus*). The occasion was not the ceremonial presentation beloved of later artists of the Empire, like Francesco Bartolozzi, in which native chiefs came forward to offer the fruits and wealth of the land to foreign explorers. Instead, on landing the Europeans made for a settlement that could be seen from the beach, only to find it deserted, the Tupinambá people having fled to the hills in fear. In the abandoned huts they discovered many parrots with purple, red, green, blue and white feathers, and calabashes full of 'fruit that looked like green pine cones but were much larger, and were filled with solid pulp, like a melon, but were much sweeter in taste and smell'.[1] In addition to its taste, they were fascinated by the appearance of the fruit and its curious quilted surface, resulting from the fact that the pineapple is not one fruit but many. Each pineapple is composed of upwards of a hundred individual berries, fused together. Much later it would be realized that a pineapple's skin is an example of a Fibonacci sequence, a pattern that draws the eyes and challenges the brain in a natural form of enchantment.

Despite these attractions, the pineapple's first sighting was a disappointment, because the aim of the voyages of the great European age of exploration that spanned the period from the beginning of the fifteenth century to the start of the seventeenth century was to find riches in the form of gold, silver, pearls, spices and precious stones. The enduring legacy of these voyages would be enrichment of another kind – the discovery of new foods like the pineapple that would change

Francesco Bartolozzi, *An Indian Priest Addressing Columbus in the Island of Cuba*, 1794, engraving. A pineapple is among the proffered fruits.

The Pyne Frute, drawing associated with John White, *c.* 1585–93.

The Pyne frute .

forever the way Europe and the rest of the world ate. However, this was far in the future.

Taking seven parrots and some of the curious fruit, Columbus and his men returned to the ships and set sail for the great island of Hispaniola, where the Admiral had made landfall on his first voyage, and where he knew gold was to be found. This was a new world in every sense, challenging all that had been known before, and everything the voyagers saw

Beauty and danger in the New World. Only the pineapple quickly overcame the colonists' fear of native foods. Parrot with snake in its beak, French, late 17th century, watercolour.

evoked wonder and fear in equal measure. Strange animals and fantastical birds made their homes in a magical setting that seemed to know no seasons. The air was perfumed with what seemed to the men to be the smell of roses and other delicate but unknown blooms. Plants produced fruits and seeds throughout the year in great abundance apparently without human aid, and from the ships the luxuriant greenery seen on the shore gave the appearance of paradise gardens.

Columbus wrote in his journal that the beauty of what he saw tempted him to stay there forever, but soon more practical considerations arose. Provisions brought from Spain began to run short and the men had not yet learned what colonists would soon discover – that native food was more digestible and suited to the tropical climate than food imported from the Old World. When the ships were near to the shore, Native Americans in canoes brought fresh water and food out to trade. Initially the men were reluctant to partake because they were convinced that the natives 'ate many things that would not only sicken, but kill us if we ate them',[2] notably snakes and iguana lizards. Only the pineapple appealed.

It was soon realized that the first fruits found on Guadeloupe had been of the small, wild sort, but there were larger cultivated pineapples that were even more delicious. Columbus's 'discovery' of the plant was only the latest encounter in a chain that stretched deep into time and the Amazon heartland, where the pineapple is believed to have originated, along with the narcotic coca plant and the cacao tree, source of chocolate. The Tupinambá people ate pineapple fresh, roasted it over the fire, dried it and made wine from it. As well as using pineapple as a food and a drink, they employed it as a medicine, made fibres for netting and plaiting from the leaves, and used it to make poison for their arrowheads.[3] By the time Columbus arrived in the New World, Native American activity over many centuries had spread the pineapple to present-day Brazil, Guiana, Colombia, parts of Central America and the West Indies. Because native methods of cultivation appeared haphazard and even invisible to Europeans, the skill the Native Americans had invested in developing different pineapple species was not appreciated. Instead, the pineapple was regarded by the newcomers as the gift of bounteous Nature, the benefaction of a divine providence.

Chivalric romances – tales of knightly quests, heroic exploits and magical enchantments – were hugely popular in the courts of Europe at the time, made accessible by the development of printing. The appetite for accounts of the discoveries was immense, and there now arose a new genre of popular writing – the literature of voyages, exploration and conquest – in which the fantastical beasts, strange beings and daring deeds of romance were projected onto the backdrop of the New World, and made real. Here, instead of dragons there were ocelots and armadillos; instead of knightly companies there were red-painted natives led by sorcerers dressed in feathers; instead of castles there were rumoured cities of gold in whose riches all hoped to share. The colonists and adventurers who followed Columbus across the Atlantic struggled to describe things that were outside all previous experience, and in their accounts the pineapple became the very symbol of all that was wondrous, exotic and desirable, the very king of fruits. The Venetian Antonio Pigafetta, who sailed around the world with Magellan, noted that 'In truth it is the most delicious fruit that can be found . . . more delicious than any apple sugared.' According to the French explorer Jean de Léry, 'the gods might luxuriate upon it and it should only be gathered by the hand of a Venus', while Sir Walter Raleigh wrote that:

> The Spaniards swear that the Pinas of Guiana was the apple that Eve tempted Adam withal: but it is true that no man can express in words the excellence of that fruit, so far does it exceed all others.

A culinary love letter to the pineapple, outstanding in the early history of food writing for its enthusiasm and length, was written by Gonzalo Fernández de Oviedo y Valdés, sent by King Ferdinand of Spain to superintend the gold foundries of Santo Domingo:

> This is one of the most beautiful fruits I have seen wherever I have been in the whole world. At least not in Spain,

After John White, Tupinambá Indians dancing; the woman holds a pineapple-shaped rattle, *c.* 1585–93, watercolour.

nor in France, nor England, nor Germany, nor Italy, nor Sicily . . . nor even though one brings in the milleruclas of Sicily and moscarela or muscadine pears. Nor all those excellent fruits which King Fernando, the first of that name in Naples collected in his gardens of the Park, the 'Paradise' and the Royal Enclosures of Naples, opinion

Maria Sibylla Merian, *Surinam Pineapple*, *c.* 1701–05, watercolour.

being that this was the prince of all orchards of most excellent fruits possessed by Christians . . . Nor Signor Ludovico Esforza, the Duke of Milan's portable orchard in small carts, whereon the trees, laden with fruit, were brought to his table and to his room. None of these nor many others I have seen had any fruits like these pines or artichokes, nor do I think there is any in the whole world to equal them in those things which I shall now tell and which are: Beauty of appearance, delicate fragrance, excellent flavour . . . it also has another great quality, which is that without any trouble to the agriculturalist it grows and sustains itself . . . When a man looks upon the beauty of this fruit he enjoys seeing its composition, the adornment with which nature painted it and made it so pleasant to the sight . . . rejoicing the other sense by a fragrance, mixed with quinces, peaches and very fine melons and surpassing in excellence all those fruits together and singly, without a doubt . . . At the time of its perfection it smells very good and gratifies this sense by its wonderful fragrance; it stands out advantageously above all other fruits. To taste it is so appetizing a thing, so delicate, that words fail to give it its true praise for this, because none of the other fruits I have mentioned can compare, by many carats, with this . . . I do not suppose that there is in the world any other of so exquisite and lovely appearance. Its flesh is . . . very satisfying to the taste.[4]

This is only a part of what he wrote. To the enamoured Oviedo, only one thing marred the perfection of the pineapple – that wine, though it be the best in the world, did not taste good after eating the fruit.

In this way, the world beyond tropical America was introduced to the pineapple. Initially, as Oviedo makes clear, the finest fruits were regarded as destined for royal tables. Brought back to Europe, pineapples enjoyed the favour of kings and aristocrats, becoming emblematic of lavish hospitality, and celebrated in art, literature, music and song. The desirability of pineapples triggered fierce competition to grow them in Europe and North America, and when this proved commercially unsuccessful the first pineapple plantations were established in the Caribbean. The golden fruit travelled the world, to Hawaii, the Atlantic and South Pacific islands, Asia and Africa, building several great colonial and modern commercial empires in the process. Supremely adaptable, the pineapple is an excellent complement to sweet, sour, bitter, salt and savoury tastes, and is equally palatable cooked, raw, dried or drunk. Today the fruit of kings has become the queen of fruits, much loved in cultures and cuisines around the globe. What follows is the edible history of how this came about.

I

Fruit of Kings

When Columbus returned to Spain from his second voyage to the New World, he brought with him gifts for the Catholic sovereigns King Ferdinand and Queen Isabella (1452–1516 and 1451–1504). The offerings consisted of gold nuggets, golden curios such as masks and ornaments made by the Indians, and exotic birds, trees, animals and plants, including a pineapple. The fruit received the ultimate royal accolade: it was eaten by Ferdinand, who promptly declared that he preferred it to all others. Taste and curiosity aside, the act was symbolic. With Columbus having claimed the West Indies for Spain, Ferdinand now made a show of consuming the fruit that represented his new possessions. The disappointed courtier who recorded the king's approval noted:

> I myself have not tasted it, for it was the only one which had arrived unspoiled, the others having rotted during the long voyage. Spaniards who have eaten them fresh plucked where they grow, speak with the highest appreciation of their delicate flavour.[1]

For the king to assert that this rare fruit was now his favourite was indeed a fine boast, a statement of his wealth and power.

Galleon tapestry, 16th century, Alcázar Palace, Seville, Spain. There is a pineapple among the fruit in the upper right corner.

However, as he had just eaten the only one in Europe, satisfying his future requirements was going to be problematic.

The finest fruits, brought from far away or grown in the king's own garden, were regarded as the perquisites of royal tables. This tradition stretched back to antiquity, when the rulers of Babylon and Assyria established celebrated gardens where they planted rare trees, fruits and flowers from distant parts of their empires, demonstrating their ability to have these things brought from faraway places, and showing their dominion over the regions from whence the plants had come. Ever since, maintaining grand gardens full of fine fruits had been the greatest of royal and princely luxuries, a source of pride and pleasure, a provider of valuable commodities for the network of royal gifting and patronage, a demonstration of might and a means of competing with fellow rulers. Yet although the palace gardens of Spain were renowned for their fruits, especially oranges, pineapples could not be made to flourish out of doors there, or anywhere else in Europe, for the pineapple required tropical warmth throughout the year. As Gonzalo Fernández de Oviedo y Valdés, the man who so loved pineapples, noted sadly:

> This is no fruit for other lands than this and some other where the climate is not so cool as in Spain . . . I have tried to ship some and, because the voyage could not be advanced, in this delay of many days they were lost; they all decayed. I tried to ship the shoots, these too were lost.[2]

For the time being, their Catholic and other majesties had to content themselves with the ships that now came from the New World laden with gold, silver, brazilwood, cochineal, sugar, pearls, precious stones and other things of great value, including the occasional pineapple which, though less than perfect, was highly prized by those grand enough to obtain it or receive it as a gift. Royalty considered the pineapple their due, for in addition to coming from faraway climes in conditions of great danger and at incalculable cost, the fruit seemed to be the very embodiment of majesty. As the French physician Pierre Pomet wrote in his *Compleat History of Drugs*, it was right to call the pineapple

> the King of Fruits because it is much the finest and best of all that are upon the Face of the Earth. It is for this Reason that the King of Kings has placed a Crown upon the Head of it, which is as an essential mark of its Royalty.[3]

In his first account of his expedition to the New World, the English explorer Sir Walter Raleigh, with courtly tact, pronounced the pineapple 'the princesse of fruits' in honour of

Elizabeth 1.[4] He could not use the word 'king', nor did he feel it politic to compare his queen to a savage fruit.

Throughout the sixteenth century, ecstatic reports flooded in from across the Atlantic, where the poorest of colonial subjects and even slaves could enjoy delicious fruits in a state of lush ripeness denied to the tables of kings, princes and the wealthy at home. In the tropics, the affinity between pineapple and sugar had been noticed, for sugar not only enhanced the fruit's sweetness but also preserved it. Preserved pineapple was being shipped to Europe from the West Indies by the late 1550s, but reports of the fresh fruits continued to tantalize, and the imported ones retained their fascination for royalty.

A pineapple is said to have been presented to James 1 of Britain in 1625, but no description of the occasion survives, although it was reported that 'It is held such a dainty fruit that King James swore it was the apple that Eve cozened Adam with.'[5] On 9 August 1661, the English diarist, botanist and courtier John Evelyn reported that: 'I saw the famous Queen-pine brought from Barbados and presented to his Majestie.' The donors were parties with interests in Barbados, then Britain's richest American possession, who were seeking more favourable trade terms for their sugar. With great wealth at their disposal, the donors settled on the pineapple rather than on plate or gold as the gift most likely to win them the attention and favour of the king, which it did. Seven years later, on 10 August 1668, a pineapple was again seen at the British court – a different strain, a 'King' pineapple – this time as part of a sumptuous banquet given by the king in honour of the ambassador sent by Louis xiv of France, an event that Evelyn was on hand to record:

> Standing by His Majesty at dinner in the presence, there was of that rare fruit called the king-pine growing in

Barbadoes and the West Indies, the first of them I had ever seen. His Majesty cut it up, was pleased to give me a piece off his own plate to taste of, but in my opinion it falls short of those ravishing varieties of deliciousness described in Captain Ligon's history and others; but possibly it might, or certainly was, much impaired in coming so far.

The pineapple is the subject of one of the more unusual British royal portraits. Dating from two years after the Whitehall banquet, it shows Charles II and the royal gardener who, on bended knee, offers the king what was long believed to be the first pineapple grown in Britain. However, as there is no evidence that pineapples had been successfully grown in Britain at this time, the portrait has been interpreted in two ways. The gardener, John Rose, was at the time employed by the family of the Duchess of Cleveland, one of the king's mistresses, and those who delighted in scandal chose to see the painting as an allegory in which the luscious fruit, representing the duchess, was being offered to the king, whose affectionate term for her was said to be 'my pineapple'. More prosaically, it is thought the pineapple shown is likely to have been an imported gift, and the portrait a testament to its rarity, value and the as yet unsatisfied appetites it aroused.

Indeed, the gulf between the pineapple's fame and the difficulty in satisfying curiosity as to its taste came to epitomize the nature of knowledge itself for the serious-minded. In his *On Human Understanding*, published in 1690, the empiricist philosopher John Locke used the pineapple to argue that true knowledge can only be based on experience. In Locke's words:

If you doubt this, see whether you can by words give anyone who has never tasted pineapple an idea of the taste of that fruit. He may approach a grasp of it by being told of its resemblance to other tastes of which he already has the ideas in his memory, imprinted there by things he has taken into his mouth; but this isn't giving him that idea by a definition, but merely raising up in him other simple ideas that will still be very different from the true taste of pineapple.[6]

Glowing reports of the pineapple continued to come in from the New World, the Englishman Richard Ligon speaking for many when he bemoaned that

> I have had many thoughts which way this fruit may be brought into England but cannot satisfy myself in any . . . that they should be brought from Barbados is impossible . . . we brought in the ship seventeen of several growths, but all rotted before we came half the way.[7]

Driven by desire, the determination took root – against all odds, reason and nature itself – to grow this tropical fruit in Europe. With a large merchant fleet, colonies in the New World and further afield, an involvement with the emerging science of botany, a keen interest in tropical plants, an appetite for imported luxuries and a susceptibility to plant manias, the Dutch took the lead.

The obsession with tulips that gripped the Netherlands during the first half of the seventeenth century, in which fortunes were lavished, won and lost on prized bulbs, created a community of highly skilled and competitive specialist gardeners well versed in the arcane arts of forcing and breeding plants in gardens specially designed to optimize growing conditions. By now, the principles of pineapple growing were well known. In the tropics, as the first explorers had reported, the

Attrib. Hendrick Danckerts (c. 1625–1680), John Rose, the King's Gardener, presenting Charles II with a pineapple, supposedly the first grown in England, at Dorney Court, Berkshire, oil on canvas.

pineapple seemed almost to grow itself. The plant looked like a thistle with sharp, spiky leaves, at the centre of which was a stalk on which the pineapple fruit grew, one fruit to a stalk, taking about ten months to a year to ripen. When the fruit was ready it was taken from the stalk, and the crown on top of the pineapple was cut off. The crown was then placed in the ground about two or three fingers deep, leaving half of it uncovered. From this, a new pineapple would grow with little further attention.

In Europe this growing method was not practicable, but the pineapple also grew shoots or slips that the Dutch had managed to nurture, and it was hoped that a way might be found to bring these to maturity. A wealthy Dutch horticulturalist named Agnes Block is credited with being the first to bring a pineapple to fruit in Europe in about 1687, on her estate at Vijverhof. She used pineapple slips from the Horticultural Garden at Leiden, which had built up a fine collection of tropical and subtropical plants with the encouragement of Prince William of Orange. It was said that the captain of every ship that left the port of Holland sailed with instructions to procure seeds and plants whenever possible. To mark her success, the proud Block caused a medal to be struck that read *Fert arsque laborque quod natura negat* (Art and Labour Bring About what Nature Cannot), and had her portrait painted with the pineapple in the garden where she had grown it.

Although Block's achievement was huge, the portrait shows that her single fruit was small and green, and cultivation on a larger scale only became possible with the development of hothouses. This followed shortly afterwards, with the first two hothouses being built in the Botanical Garden, Amsterdam and the Chelsea Physic Garden, London. Indoor cultivation in Britain received further royal impetus when Prince William of Orange came to the throne as William III and ordered greenhouses to be built at Hampton Court Palace, London, importing exotic plants from the Netherlands to fill them. The Dutch pioneered the design and use of hothouses and indoor gardening, in buildings where heat was maintained by ingenious means at enormous cost, making this an enterprise for royalty, the nobility and gentry, and the wealthy new merchant and professional classes. Here the art of growing pineapple plants from slips was perfected. The European elite sent their gardeners to study Dutch methods and construction, and to buy Dutch pineapple plants – not slips but plants that had been brought to the stage where crowns had developed – which they hoped to ripen in newly built hothouses of their own.

The hothouses were the technological marvels of their day, employing complex stoves, elaborate flues, under-floor ovens and heated plant stands to imitate the tropics in cold climes, all maintained by skilled craftsmen, carpenters, plantsmen and nurserymen rather than ordinary gardeners. Dedicated structures soon developed, notably orangeries for orange trees, and pineries or pine houses for pineapples, along with specialized techniques. 'Pineapple pits' were brick-lined pits filled with fresh horse manure and chopped tanning bark covered with a glazed protective covering that could be removed for ventilation. The pits generated heat in the manner of a compost heap, providing a hot bed for the young pineapples, but the manure and chopped bark had to be changed at intervals to keep up the internal temperature. The pineapples, in individual pots, were put into the manure, taken out and drained, rotated, plunged back into the manure, sprayed with milk-warm water and generally pampered to an extent that almost defied belief.

Although the Dutch pioneered the technique, Britain and France were the two European countries that pursued the cultivation of pineapples with a spirit that amounted to obsession. In Britain, the cost of a young pineapple plant purchased to be brought to fruit in a hothouse with no guarantee of success was between four and five shillings, at a time when a common labourer was fortunate if he earned £15 a year.[8] Even under the best conditions, it took some two years or more for pineapples grown in this way to become large enough to fruit; longer than in the tropics. The exorbitant cost of supporting the plants, the hothouses and the people who maintained them heightened the reputation of the pineapple as a status symbol and object of desire. It was galling to hear reports that, out in the tropical colonies, pineapples were so common that they were disdained. In colonial Surinam there were many different

Maria Sibylla Merian, *Pineapple and Insects*, *c.* 1701–05, watercolour.

kinds, growing spontaneously without cultivation in such abundance that 'on many estates they serve as common food for hogs'.[9] In Sierra Leone and Formosa (Taiwan) they grew wild by the roadside, while in Ceylon (Sri Lanka) fine pineapples could be bought for a penny or less.[10]

Collecting rare plants and displaying an interest in natural history were regarded as the proper pursuits of aristocrats and the rich – both male and female – equivalent to the collecting of art and antiquities. Explorations were revealing the world as a living cabinet of curiosities, inhabited by brilliant butterflies, ornate caterpillars, marvellous flora and above all the pineapple, as depicted by Maria Sibylla Merian in around 1703.

Among the elite, interest in pineapple growing reached fever pitch, as did competition. Gifted plantsmen could command huge fees, and young pineapple plants were traded between friends and stolen from enemies. Bribery, horticultural secrecy and sabotage were commonplace. Although the hothouses could be visited, pineapples under cultivation could not be shown off out of doors in the way prize peaches and plums could, so the gardens and parks that surrounded palaces and stately homes now sprouted strange fruit. Stone pineapples large and small appeared as statuary and decorations on the facades and roofs of hothouses, and topiary specialists trimmed bushes and trees into the ornamental shapes of pineapples, all announcing the owner's involvement with this kingly fruit.

In France, the passion for exotic botany – transplanting indigenous species to Europe for cultivation and ornamental display – was equally intense, perfectly suiting the national penchant for imposing order on nature, as seen in the highly formal gardens at the palace of Versailles. Here, from the early 1660s, Louis xiv (1638–1715), the 'Sun King', deployed an army of architects, engineers, artists, plantsmen and gardeners to

Stone pineapple fountain. Emblematic of wealth and luxury, pineapples were favoured motifs in architectural design and interior decoration.

create a garden that was a grand political statement in the manner of the ancient Assyrian kings. Broad avenues, ornamental parterres, statues, grottos, terraces, fountains and canals astonished the eye, and promenades through this royal pleasure garden were both a favoured activity of the courtiers, and a means whereby the king was able to impress on foreign visitors the might and majesty of France. The king had a formal itinerary drawn up to ensure that favoured visitors and diplomatic emissaries saw the gardens to their best advantage, and were properly entertained along the way:

> Leaving the Apartment of the Seven Baths, go to the middle of the Orangery, and then to the side of the

Labyrinth, and pause there to consider the orange trees and the Chateau . . . go on to the Marais where there will be fruit and ices.[11]

The Potager du Roi – the royal kitchen garden with beds and greenhouses full of out-of-season fruits and vegetables – was the king's special pride, for here he could demonstrate his triumph over the natural horticultural calendar and satisfy his own appetites for the delicious and rare. The reputation of the pineapple had preceded it to court – Madame de Maintenon, the king's morganatic wife, who had tasted the pineapple in her youth in Martinique, described its taste as being between an apricot and a melon. According to an apocryphal tale, when first presented with a fresh pineapple, Louis xiv was so eager to try it that he bit into it unskinned, cutting his lip.

Sugar was the other great edible luxury of the age. The confluence of unprecedented supplies of precious sugar and the development of elite greenhouses and hothouses resulted in the emergence of fine fruit confectionery, one of the glories of French grand cuisine. Sugar and fruit confectionery was

French sugar bowl with pineapple finial, late 18th century.

regarded by many as the highest form of culinary art, and because of the ingredients the dessert course was the most expensive part of an elite repast. Banquets at Versailles in the time of Louis xiv consisted of a succession of courses, the last of which – the dessert course – was considered so important that it was served in a separate room. Here confectionery, fresh and sugared fruits, sugar sculptures, wafers, macaroons, marchpanes and meringues were displayed in magnificent pyramids, tableaux and arrangements that the guests would circle and admire, before helping themselves to sugar plums, candied currants with tincture of raspberries, caramel cherries, pastilles of figs, green gooseberry jellies, and much more. The word 'banquet', which now denotes a grand meal, comes from the term 'fruit banquet', which is what the dessert course was once called. Chocolate has so overwhelmed the modern palate that it is difficult to imagine the delights of the fruit-based confectionery of the past, or the dizzying cost of sweets made from hothouse fruits and sugar that was considered almost as precious as gold. Jam or 'confiture' was such a treat that it was served in bowls and eaten by the spoonful.

As the rarest and costliest of fruits, the pineapple reigned supreme over the dessert course, but only symbolically to begin with. Although it was introduced into the Sun King's gardens in 1702, success proved elusive. Thus carved and gilded pineapples crowned the pyramids of sweetmeats, and pineapples made of sugar served as centrepieces on dessert tables, while efforts were redoubled to grow the fruit in France. However, preserved pineapple came to the court from the colonies, and this was used in the most spectacular of royal desserts – the ice creams and sorbets that the king adored and for which Versailles became renowned. Ice and pineapple were luxuries of the highest kind, and pineapple ice cream was therefore the perfect dessert for a king.

Jean Lepautre, *Banquet Table with Sweets at Versailles*, 18 July 1668, print.

It was not until the reign of the Sun King's successor, Louis XV (1710–1774), that the pineapple was successfully cultivated indoors at Versailles. Abbé Pluche, a priest who wrote a wonderfully gossipy, popular natural history, reported that the king had received two suckers of a pineapple,

> although they were almost withered at that time, and had not any roots. The heart, however, was good, and they happened to take. But though the fruit they produced could not be advanced to its proper maturity, yet two suckers that were preserved from the putrefaction and danger of the others produced, in the year 1733, two pineapples.[12]

The day the king received the pineapples was considered worthy of recording – 28 December. His Majesty tasted one, found it excellent, and had the second cut for the benefit of those persons he thought fit to share it with. All pronounced it excellent. A hothouse on the Dutch model was built at

Versailles that could accommodate 800 plants. The nobility now took up pineapple growing, and hothouses were constructed at chateaux across France, just as on estates in England.

Pineapples now began to be fully incorporated into the dessert repertoire. Confectioners had several ways of boiling sugar – smooth, pearled, blown, feathered, cracked and caramel – many varieties of sugar and a battery of fruit-working techniques, all of which they used to transform the pineapple into a royal selection of sweets. Louis xv was partial to desserts, and he also put the French royal passion for pineapples to practical use. On the *qui vive* for a new mistress, the king's attention

Albert Eckhout, *Still-life with Watermelon, Pineapple and Other Fruit*, *c.* 1640, oil on canvas.

was drawn to a married commoner, later known to history as Madame de Pompadour. The challenge was how to become better acquainted with the lady under the watchful eyes of the court. The wedding of the Dauphin in 1745 presented the king with an opportunity. Arranging a grand masquerade ball where he could mingle with the courtiers incognito, the king waited until all the guests – including his intended, dressed as a shepherdess – were present, then entered with his companions. All were dressed identically from head to toe, as yew trees trimmed in the shape of pineapples. The symbolism was clear – one of these bushes was royal, but which one? It was impossible to tell them apart, and in the confusion the king was able to become better acquainted with the shepherdess in plain view of the court. Shortly afterwards she became his mistress, and she remained fond of pineapples ever after.[13]

Back in Britain, pineapple fever raged unabated, as did the temperatures in the hothouses, which entered common parlance. Describing being overcome at a dance, someone might say, 'we had got above pineapple heat, and I became sick and oppressed. I asked leave to get out.'[14] From the 1760s, treatises on pineapple cultivation began to appear, written by the gardeners of the Duke of Portland, Baroness Rothschild and the Marquis of Hertford among others. These merely added fuel to the ongoing debates about the relative virtues of different kinds of soil and manure, of competing designs of stove and pit, of the advantages of heating with steam or hot water, about whether the potted plants should be transplanted to indoor beds after a while, and whether the sizes of pots should change with the season. The University of Oxford established a fine hothouse in its botanical gardens where pineapples were 'raised to great perfection'. At the height of pineapple mania, it is estimated that each hothouse pine brought to maturity cost some £80 to produce, £1,890 or $3,000 in today's money.[15]

Trade card of Henry Scott, a gardener at Weybridge noted for growing ananas or pineapples, 1754.

Not surprisingly, critics decried the pineapple as the very embodiment of social inequality and gluttony, a luxury fruit produced at enormous cost when many were hungry. However, for all the effort and expense lavished on its cultivation, the pineapple remained something of a culinary mystery, better known by sight and reputation than by taste on account of its rarity.

The pineapple continued to trouble philosophers, for as David Hume complained, 'We cannot form to ourselves a just idea of the pineapple, without actually having tasted it.'[16] However, most people's interest in the pineapple was more worldly. The fruit's distinctive appearance made it a natural symbol of wealth, extravagance and the exotic. Just as stone and topiary pineapples had appeared on the landscape, so the

Der Esser or *The Glutton*, German satirical print of a fat man surrounded by culinary delicacies, including a lobster and a pineapple, *c.* 1815–20.

pineapple now flourished in the domestic interior. Pineapple finials sprouted on furniture, and pineapples were carved in wood and given places of honour on gilded mirrors and above doors. Pineapples appeared as teapots, and on tea caddies,

Pineapple grown by traditional means at the restored Lost Gardens of Heligan, Cornwall.

creamers, honey and jam pots, dessert dishes, jelly and butter moulds, and fine silver, while pineapple patterns embellished wallpaper, fabrics, crochet and lace.

Pineapple decorations also appeared on the elaborate hairstyles of the period, which rose to great heights, embellished by decorative status symbols. As the culinary anthropologist Sophie Coe put it, 'the pineapple became not just a fruit, but the embodiment of everything the nobility liked to think it stood for'.[17] As such, it was taken up in every way by anyone with social aspirations.

When a hothouse pineapple was successfully brought to fruit, a terrible choice arose – should it be displayed, to enhance status, or should it be eaten, to satisfy curiosity?

Sometimes both could be achieved. Those who grew their own pineapples made a great show of displaying them in lavish arrangements at grand dinners, then having them cut and handed round for their guests' pleasure, so the pineapple came to denote lavish hospitality. The wealthy could purchase a pineapple to enhance their reputations as hosts, and dramatists used the fruit to satirize high society. In *The Rivals*, Richard Brinsley Sheridan's Mrs Malaprop describes a character as 'the very pineapple of politeness' when she means to say 'pinnacle'. Those who could not afford to grow or buy their own but still wanted to impress could rent a pineapple to display during their entertainments, in the same way that they could rent fine china and silver. To satisfy taste, they could serve their guests pineapple sweets ordered in from the elite confectioners that were opening in major cities, utilizing Britain's own lavish supplies of colonial sugar. In London the most renowned confectioner was Domenico Negri, who in the 1760s opened his confectionery shop at the Sign of the Pineapple in Berkeley Square, an establishment that was later

Staffordshire pineapple ware, probably from the factory of Thomas Whieldon, *c.* 1760.

Fruit Stall, satirical print of a woman's hairstyle embellished with hothouse fruits and surmounted by a pineapple, *c.* 1777.

FRUIT STALL.

to become Gunter's, the famous society *maison de thé*, noted for its ices, including tea ice cream, ginger water ice and pineapple ice cream. Recipes for pineapple chips, syrup and ice cream by the master confectioner Frederick Nutt, who worked for Negri, are included in this book (see pp. 131–2).

In the cult of the pineapple, royalty continued to lead the way. George III (1738–1820), remembered today as the king who lost the American colonies, was known in his own time as Farmer George on account of his passion for agriculture and agronomy and his interest in exotic plants, which he shared with his friend Joseph Banks, the Pacific explorer and naturalist. Under George III, the royal gardens at Windsor flourished, supplying fruits to all the other London palaces from four separate kitchen gardens in Windsor Great Park, each with its own pineries, vineries, orangeries and forcing houses.[18] The produce of the royal hothouses was shown to advantage in grand dessert courses, as described in this newspaper account of a banquet George held at Windsor Castle.

> The ornamental parts of the confectionery were numerous and splendid. There were temples four feet high, in which the different stories were sweetmeats. The various orders of architecture were also done with inimitable taste . . . the dessert comprehended all the hothouse was competent to afford – and indeed more than it was thought art could produce at this time of the year. There were a profusion of pineapples, strawberries of every denomination, peaches, nectarines, apricots, cherries of each kind, from the Kentish to the Morella, plums and raspberries, with the best and richest preserved fruits, as well as those that are in syrup.[19]

The pineapple reached the pinnacle of royal luxe under George III's son, the Prince Regent, later George IV (1762–1830). At his coronation banquet in 1821 – the most lavish in British history – a prize-winning pineapple that weighed ten and a half pounds was among the delicacies served to the king. Noted for his extravagance in an age of ostentation, the Prince Regent's memorial is the Brighton Pavilion, his pleasure palace by the sea. On the outside this architectural fantasy was a melange of Mughal domes, minarets and pagodas. On the inside it was a flamboyance of chinoiserie. All the walls, ceilings, canopies and columns were embellished with dragons, phoenixes, strange fish and rare plants including bamboo, bananas and pineapples. These were portrayed in gold, silver

John Agar, hand-coloured print showing the banqueting room at Brighton Pavilion in 1824, with a banquet in progress. Pineapples feature in the decorative scheme and on the menu.

and vivid shades of Chinese red, yellow, blue and jade green, lit with silken lanterns and crystal chandeliers, reaching a crescendo in the magnificent banqueting room.

The Prince Regent so relished his food that a quarter of the ground floor of the Pavilion was given over to the royal kitchens and offices, including five rooms dedicated to pastry and confectionery. The feasts held at the Pavilion in the remarkable Banqueting Room were known for their elaborateness and length. Dinner was served at 6 p.m. and went on for hours, with between 40 and 70 dishes presented, according to the occasion.[20] The services of a fine French chef were considered essential to grand dining, and for a time the Prince Regent was cooked for by the most renowned chef of the day, Marie-Antoine Carême, who created for him the opulent royal pineapple dessert *Pouding d'Ananas á la Royale*. A rich melange of preserved cherries, pistachio nuts, pears, pineapple and whipped cream frozen together in a mould, it was perfectly suited to the Prince Regent's tastes and the fantastical setting of the Pavilion.

With the pineapple now established as the fruit of kings in Europe, it is time to return to the New World, where the fruit's fortunes were very different.

2

Mapping the Pineapple

An exhaustive tome on pineapple cultivation written in 1847 began:

> it is found wild in the tropical latitudes of America, Africa and Asia. Tradition says that being native of the first of the above named of the earth's quarters, it was then exported to the others.[1]

By that time the pineapple had indeed circled the globe, and to map the pineapple is to chart the history of exploration and empire.

Discovery for its own sake was not the aim of the great voyages. Certainly adventure was to be had and fortunes were to be made, but there was a larger design. The full sequence went expedition–exploration–exploitation–enrichment–empire, culminating in a 'plantation economy'. Once claimed, the newly discovered lands were transformed into colonies whose riches could be sent back to the mother country. Networks of colonies belonging to the same country constituted an empire, hopefully self-sufficient unto itself, linked by trade and culture. In the first instance, 'plantation' referred to people rather than plants; the 'planting' in new soil of colonial settlers and

Early English exploration: a map of the East Coast of North America with the arms of Sir Walter Raleigh, drawn by John White, 1585–93. There were attempts to grow pineapples in the Virginia colony.

settlements to produce goods for export. In some colonies gold, silver and indigenous spices were the major exports but, in many more, exports would in time consist of crops grown intensively on specialized agricultural plantations, the best known being those devoted to sugar.

Generally, wherever sugar thrived, so did the pineapple. It was to prove a fateful marriage. It has always been the case, as the noted food writer and gourmet André Simon wrote, that

> A fully-ripe pineapple, neither cooked nor flavoured, is the finest dessert fruit grown in tropical and sub-tropical countries, and ever so much better than any of the made-up pineapple dishes.[2]

Sugar cane and pineapple together on a Cuban stamp.

However, unless pineapple could be had fresh from the field, it would almost always be combined with sugar, and made into a drink or something sweet to eat.

On his second voyage, Columbus arrived with a large complement of settlers, animals, plants and seeds that were to take root in the New World. Finding themselves with dwindling supplies of what they considered the necessities of life – wine, biscuit, garlic, vinegar and cheese[3] – and seeing that the plants and animals they brought with them did not flourish, the early Spaniards turned to the natives for fresh foods. As Oviedo, the man who loved pineapples, wrote, 'this fruit is one of the principal reasons why the few Christians who live in these lands can survive among these barbarous people'.[4]

Fresh provisions were first obtained through barter, then through forced labour, with the Europeans obliging the natives to grow food plants for them. The pattern was repeated in what became the Portuguese, French, Dutch and British tropical colonies, initially in South and Central America and the Caribbean, and later further afield. The Indian legacy – the ghost in the name – lives on in the word *ananas* and variations, the Tupi-Guarani term for the pineapple, which today is used in most languages except in Spanish, in which the fruit is called *piña,* echoing the first descriptions of it as being like a pine cone, and in English. In Brazil and Portugal the pineapple is called *abacaxi*, another Indian word that refers to the fragrance of the fruit. Although the pineapple's perfume has now been largely bred out of it, many early explorers and travellers commented on it, the German Alexander von Humboldt writing of the Upper Orinoco that

> the humid evening air is filled far and wide with the fragrance of the ripe *ananas*. The stalks of the pineapples, swelling with rich juice, rise between the lowly herbs of the meadow, and the golden fruit is seen shining at a distance from under its leafy crown of bluish-green.

Native food was needed for the settlements, and also to provision the ships that touched at the New World, then sailed on in search of new territories, braving seas that were no longer a barrier. This first wave of exploration led by the Portuguese and Spanish carried the pineapple around the world. While some pineapples travelled as precious cargo bound for the royal courts and elaborate hothouses of Europe, many others were carried on voyages across largely uncharted oceans, providing crews with much-needed fresh food and a degree of protection against scurvy. There were three main sea routes along which the pineapple travelled from the New World. The Portuguese, then in the process of building their empire and trading network, took the pineapple from Brazil to the Atlantic island of St Helena in

1505 and other Atlantic islands shortly afterwards, to Madagascar in about 1548, to southern India in 1550 and to China through the Portuguese colony of Macao. By 1602 the pineapple was being cultivated in Portuguese Guinea on the West African coast, a centre of the slave trade, later spreading throughout West Africa.

In their rivalry over the Spice Islands, both Spain and Portugal reached the western Pacific islands, and from here pineapples spread across the South Pacific. The third route, established by the Spanish, was the famed Pacific transit that linked Acapulco in Mexico with Manila in the Philippines. Once a year starting in 1565, the fabled Manila Galleons would ply this route, transporting Mexican silver to trade for spices, silks and other goods from the East, and also carrying pineapples. The route of the galleons took the shape of a giant eye, with the outward voyage arcing across the North Pacific and the return journey going south along the equator, riding the winds and tides. In this way the galleons missed what was at the centre of the eye, the as-yet undiscovered islands of Hawaii, where the pineapple would one day find its perfect home – but that was centuries away. For now, the pineapple settled in the Philippines, and moved on to Java by 1599, to Singapore by 1637, to Taiwan by 1650, and to Assam, Burma and Thailand by 1700. The Dutch, with less extensive colonial possessions, took the pineapple from Java to the Cape of Good Hope in 1660.[5]

With remarkable rapidity, the pineapple had become a global tropical fruit within 200 years of Columbus's first sighting of it, in an age when travel was slow and extremely difficult. Sometimes the transplantation was planned, but more often it seems to have been accidental, with the hardy discarded crowns taking root in amenable soil, then becoming naturalized, and thriving so well that later travellers assumed that pineapples

WADERS.

They are soil slaves, in rank are lower than the Mooly Corawers, but the people of the high caste suppose that on seing their lump turning light at night in their huts the whole success of the day next will succeed in good.

Waders: the pineapple on the Malabar Coast, South India. Company school, *c.* 1850, watercolour.

were native to the many regions in which they were now found. When the Jesuit priest Michal Boym visited southern China in 1656, the pineapple was already so common there that he assumed it was a native and included it in *Flora Simensis*, the first Western work on Chinese plants. This error bore artistic fruit in the form of tapestries made at Beauvais and elsewhere for the European elite that showed highly romanticized scenes of Chinese pineapple harvests.[6]

Immediately appreciated as a fresh fruit, pineapples were incorporated into other dishes and entered the cuisines of their new locales. In organoleptic terms, the pineapple's great contribution has been the unique 'sweet-and-sour' taste developed to its greatest extent in Southeast Asian cookery but now found globally in main dishes, drinks, desserts and a wide range of sambals, chutneys, syrups, vinegars and salsas. In some cases the pineapple would also enter the economies of its new homelands, but that would be in the future. Initially, like a sleeper, the pineapple remained quietly in place, awaiting technological developments that would enable it to play a part in larger events, as was happening in the New World, to which we now return.

A curious feature of most modern histories of the age of discovery is the way they ignore the problems of provisioning, despite the fact that a preoccupation with food runs through all the contemporary European accounts of New World colonization. The early explorers and settlers thought, talked and wrote endlessly about food – about the home foods they missed, whether their supplies would run out and when ships with new provisions might arrive. However, they mainly wrote about their dislike and fear of the native foods.[7] In the Caribbean and Brazil, the main staple was cassava or manioc, which was poisonous until it was subjected to laborious processing. In Mexico the chillies were diabolically hot and the maize needed to be treated with lime and sometimes fermented before consumption. In Peru the many varieties of potato at first seemed inedible, and everywhere people ate strange birds, fish, mammals, plants and insects completely

48

outside European experience, among them armadillos, snakes, iguanas, water bugs and the *cuy* or guinea pig.

When the Europeans first saw chocolate, they did not dare to drink it. Apart from experiencing feelings of distaste for these strange foods, the explorers and settlers feared that they would destroy their health and rob them of their European identity and very nature, transforming them into natives. Both Columbus and Hernán Cortés (1485–1547), who overthrew the Aztec Empire, had to force their men to eat Indian food. Bernal Díaz del Castillo, who fought under Cortés, complained bitterly about the rations, calling them: 'our misery of maize cakes, *aji* or pepper, *tunas* (cactus fruit) and herbs'.[8] However, Díaz also recorded with approval that the first time the Spaniards heard of 'the name and power of the great Montezuma' was at a banquet given by a native chief who served them 'many chickens of the land' and pineapples.[9]

Out of all the new foods and fruits, only the pineapple met with general European approval. The delight with which the early settlers in the Caribbean embraced the pineapple was captured by the Englishman Richard Ligon:

> When we gather them, we leave some of the stalk to take hold by, and when we come to eat them, we first cut off the crown and send that to be planted, and then with a knife pare off the rind which is so beautiful that it grieves us to rob the fruit of such an ornament, nor would we do so but to enjoy the precious substance it contains; like a Thief that breaks a beautiful cabinet which we would forebear to do, but for the treasure he expects to find within.[10]

In addition to savouring what Ligon described as the taste 'between two extremes of sharp and sweet [wherein lies the relish and flavour of all fruits that are excellent', the settlers

– who suffered constantly from ill health and digestive upsets – soon discovered what the Indians had long known. As they widely reported, the pineapple

> admirably recreates and exhilarates the Spirits and comforts the Heart; it also fortifies the Stomack, cureth queasiness and causeth Appetite; it gives present ease to such as are troubled with the Stone or stoppage of Urine, nay it destroys the effects of Poison.[11]

Once the new settlers were in place, colonial cuisines in which the pineapple played a part began to develop. These emerging foodways were differentiated by the specificities of location and climate, local foods, whether or not European plants and animals flourished there, and the culture of the home country. The most extreme example of a European

Perfectly ripe pineapple slices.

The Rede or Net: Brazilian men carrying a white woman in a hammock on a pole, followed by a woman carrying a basket of pineapples on her head. A man carrying cut sugar cane is passing by on the other side, 1821, hand-coloured print.

cuisine 'gone native' arose in the Portuguese colony of Brazil. Portuguese settlement of Brazil began in earnest in 1531–2, when the attention of the Portuguese began to shift from the Asian arena to the Atlantic. The area chosen for intensive settlement was the tropical northeast, where it soon became apparent that European crops would not flourish. The need to produce profitable exports was pressing and – in the absence of gold, silver and spices – the only candidate was sugar. Sugar cane from the Atlantic islands was among the plants brought to the New World by Columbus in 1493, on the voyage during which he 'discovered' the pineapple. Unlike many European imports sugar cane thrived, and the first sugar was exported to Europe from Spanish Santo Domingo in the Caribbean in around 1516.[12] Prices and demand soared and sugar became the new edible colonial gold.

William Havell, scene of women purchasing bananas, pineapples and melons on the Braganza shore, Rio de Janeiro, 1827, watercolour.

The establishment of northeast Brazil as a major centre of sugar production resulted in a greater reliance on native foodways and methods there than in other colonies. Because the northeast was not suitable for maize or European crops that could support a large body of cane workers – Europeans, natives and slaves brought from Africa – manioc, which only the natives could process, became the staple. In time this became a source of Brazilian identity and pride. A cosmopolitan cuisine developed, prepared by native cooks who fused local and European dishes, methods and ingredients, and later incorporated African elements. Unusually for the period, this northeast Brazilian creole cuisine was not just for the lower orders, but also for the plantation aristocracy who lived in the great houses – the *casas grandes*. It was in the shadow of these mansions and the sugar mills that the intensely sweet candies and cakes came into being that are one of the glories of Brazilian cuisine.[13]

Pernambuco was reckoned to be where the best sugar came from, and also the best candies and cakes, exquisite creations sweet to the point of being cloying, presented in elaborate arrangements on hand-cut paper doilies. Pineapple was chopped into fine tapioca *mingaus* and baked into meltingly moist manioc-based pineapple cakes, but the greatest delicacies were sweets in the northeastern style, such as *doce de abacaxi pernambuco* – pineapples picked when they were swollen to bursting with juice, peeled, boiled in white wine, dried, put into rapidly boiling Pernambuco sugar syrup, drained and cut into pieces. These were not mere imitations of European confectionery. Food spoiled rapidly in the intense tropical heat, and before the coming of the Europeans and the introduction of sugar cane, the natives had known how to preserve fruit using honey and sugar made from the palm, sweet potato and pineapple.

In Mexico, by contrast, as soon as 'the conquerors began to metamorphose into settlers',[14] the native foodways taken up out of necessity in the early days were put aside by the colonial aristocracy. Instead of chilli stews, pepper and herb sauces, maize tamales and tortillas stuffed with beans, tomatoes, squash, meat, fish, avocado and smoked chilli, the colonial elite demanded food in the European manner, or as close to it as conditions allowed, as a means of emphasizing its class identity.[15]

Of the native foods, only game, fruits and large birds – all of which could be prepared and presented in a European fashion – were acceptable to the elite. The Aztecs had relished fruit, appreciating both the sweet and the sour, and as the pineapple combined the two, it had been much esteemed. Pineapple now found a similarly honoured place on aristocratic colonial tables, both fresh and made into confectionery. At the time confectionery was considered a medicine as well

Colonial heritage: popular throughout Central and South America, European-style custard flan, served with pineapple and other fruits.

as a food, good for cleansing the system, stimulating the blood and settling the digestion, qualities the pineapple also had. Sugar was most often taken in the form of syrup, candied fruits and fruit conserves. Pineapple continued to play a part in native and emerging mestizo cuisine, seen today in traditional dishes like *mancha manteles de cerdo*[16] or 'tablecloth stainer' – a stew of pork, three kinds of chilli, tomatoes and fruit including pineapple – and in culinary (re-)inventions like 'Chicken Oaxaca', a chicken, chilli and pineapple concoction named in honour of the state that is currently one of Mexico's largest pineapple producers, as well as in modern Mexican fusion dishes like quesadillas with pineapple salsa.

Fruit confectionery using the pineapple spread throughout Spanish South America, including Peru. The pineapple had not grown in Peru until it was introduced there by the Spaniards, and the following seventeenth-century recipe shows the reach of the Spanish colonial trading network, for the almonds and raisins would have come across the Atlantic from Spain, and the cinnamon from across the Pacific, brought by the Manila Galleons:

> The nuns of Huanaco have a singular method of preparing pineapple sweets, which they do in the following manner. First they clean them, then they cook them in water to rid them of their sourness and stickiness. In this condition they remove the core, which is about half of the flesh, which they grind with almonds, raisins, sugar and cinnamon, forming a smooth filling, with which they fill the hollow of the fruit which has been previously cooked in sugar, and afterwards they give this two or three baths of sugar, which results in the most delicate pineapple sweets, weighing three to six pounds each.[17]

Down in the islands of the Caribbean, sugar production passed out of the control of the Spanish and into the hands of the French and British. The native population of the islands declined precipitously in the colonial period, leaving behind little but their favoured way of consuming the pineapple – by grilling it over an open fire, a technique the early Spanish called *barbacoa,* the origins of the modern 'barbecue'.

The French established sugar plantations on Guadaloupe (where Columbus had 'discovered' the pineapple) in the early seventeenth century, and later on in Martinique. The development of the premier British sugar colony, Barbados, began in 1627, and Jamaica was taken from Spain by Britain in

1655. The newly established plantations on the sugar islands were worked by slaves from Africa for the benefit of an emerging elite of planters that established an enviable way of life. Writing from Spanish Town, Jamaica in 1740, one traveller noted that

> They live here after a very gay manner, it is surprising to see the number of coaches and chariots which are perpetually plying, besides those which belong to private persons; they have frequent balls, and have lately got a playhouse, where they maintain a set of extraordinary good actors. In short they live as happily as if they were within the verge of the British Court.[18]

It was in the sugar planters' grand houses that Caribbean colonial cuisine came into being. Despite the desire to maintain European foodways, this was not possible on the islands where few European crops flourished and where, in any case, all agricultural effort was spent on sugar rather than on diversification. Pineapples were grown privately in gardens, on small holdings and in places where sugar would not thrive, and continued to flourish in the wild, but here, for now, sugar was king.

With sugar constantly to hand, the making of *confitures* or preserves of tropical fruit – especially pineapple – was one of the first offshoots of the sugar industry, with consignments sent back to the elite tables of the home countries. Beyond that, French cuisine on the islands aimed to be more elaborate than the British, but in both cases it boiled down to using native foods in as European a manner as possible, even as African elements crept into the cooking.

At least for the planters, it was a gracious and leisurely world of cool verandahs, gardens aflame with bright bougainvillea and hibiscus, picnics by day and, by night, dining in

Satirical print of plantation dining with cigars, drink and pineapples on the table, 1802.

rooms with long windows open to catch the breeze. The classic Caribbean colonial dinner would usually begin with soup, in an attempt to hang on to European formalities. It then proceed to a tropical fish course – possibly flying fish, considered a great delicacy – and on to a roast flanked not with European vegetables, but with yams, eddoes, sweet potatoes, avocado pears and bread fruit. Dessert usually consisted of a wealth of tropical fruits – pineapples, guavas, soursops, bananas, mangoes, China oranges and many more – which were refreshing in the sultry heat and served in abundance.

Away from the great houses, the slaves also enjoyed pineapple when they could get it, eating it fresh, barbecued and pickled, and using the juice to tenderize tough meat before flavouring it with native allspice, in a technique that later became known to the world as 'jerk'.

Visiting the plantations of the Caribbean became a new Grand Tour for adventurous young men of good family, and in 1751–2 one such came to Barbados, recording in his diary that there he saw more fruit upon the table than he had ever seen. 'There are many delicious fruits', he wrote, 'but the pineapple, China orange and avocado . . . nothing pleases my taste as much as these'.[19] This young man was George Washington, the future first president of what were then Britain's thirteen colonies in North America. Washington never forgot his island experiences, and at his presidential inauguration 38 years later, he insisted on having a barrel of Barbados rum for his guests.

In North America, the British had achieved the *beau idéal* of all colonizing nations – to impose a template of the Old World on the New, most especially in the northern colonies where the climate closely corresponded to that of the home country. Here they had successfully transplanted British animals, plants

Jamaican jerk chicken with rice, a colonial classic. The pineapple can be cooked with the chicken, served separately as a salsa or used in a marinade.

Victor Facchina, *George Washington*, first president of the United States of America, 1930, drawing.

and foodways, which they were intent on maintaining. As in Spanish South America, there was an initial phase of having to rely on native food and aid, but within a decade of the first British settlement of what became the New England colony of Massachusetts in 1620, European grain was being planted alongside Indian corn, allowing a replication of the common British diet of the period – stews, pottages, puddings, porridges and gruels eaten with bread and with honest English fruits – apple, pear, plum, quince and cherry.[20] Britain had, however, also transplanted the class system, which took root and flourished in the southernmost colonies, far away in every sense from the puritanical north.

Britain's first attempt at New World colonization had been at Jamestown in the Virginia colony in 1607. Here the climate was humid and subtropical, and an attempt to grow sugar there was made in 1619. This failed, as did an attempt to grow pineapples, of which early colonist William Strachey reported sadly that 'the roots of the delicious Indian-Pina, set in a sandy place, thrived and continued life . . . until the cold winter and weeds choked it.' Further efforts were made to establish the pineapple in Virginia, all unsuccessful, which only served to increase the appetite for it.

If tropical plants failed in Virginia, the plantation system did not. Virginia planters with large holdings in land and slaves grew rich on tobacco, America's first great agricultural cash crop. While the culture of New England was that of yeomen and hardy farmers, Virginia culture – from which George Washington sprang – was aristocratic or gentrified, replicating in every regard the elite tastes of home, including a passion for the pineapple. Throughout the eighteenth century, the *Virginia Gazette* regularly announced the arrival of ships from the West Indies; in August 1768 a ship from New

Pineapple pie, a contemporary version of an American colonial favourite.

Providence arrived with 100 dozen pineapples and 30,000 limes.[21] The Governor's palace in colonial Williamsburg had cuisine as fine as any in Europe, and over the course of 1770 the then governor, Baron de Botetourt, ordered 65 pineapples at an average cost of one shilling and eightpence each to serve to his guests at banquets, at a time when a young journeyman craftsman was paid between £25 and £35 a year, each pound sterling being worth twenty shillings.[22] Governor Botetourt was charged with smoothing relations between the Virginia planters and Britain, so his lavish hospitality was strategic.

Pineapples were used for table displays, and were a favourite in contemporary recipes such as that for pineapple pudding given in *Thomas Jefferson's Cook Book* (see recipe, p. 133), and pineapple pies and tarts. As in Britain, pineapples were incorporated into domestic decoration, appearing on furniture, wallpaper, fabrics, silver, china and the architectural details of grand colonial homes. Even today, Colonial Williamsburg is noted for its fine Christmas displays and wreaths using pineapples, now widely imitated.

In both the New England and southern colonies, pineapples appeared on the tables of the wealthy, both as something to eat and as high-status object of display, a tradition that has continued down the centuries. 'The marriage of Washington's best-looking young senator to Washington's prettiest inquiring photographer'[23] – John Fitzgerald Kennedy and Jacqueline Bouvier – took place in 1953. At this high-society wedding of the year, the wedding luncheon consisted of fruit cup served in a pineapple shell, creamed chicken and ice cream sculpted to resemble roses, along with a five-tier wedding cake four feet tall.[24]

When George Washington ordered three dozen West Indian pineapples for a grand dinner he gave in 1774, he was doing no more than others of his background did when seeking to impress their peers, obtaining the fruit through sources of supply that were by then well established. The American colonies were part of the triangular trade route that began in the seventeenth century and matured in the eighteenth, linking Britain, Africa and the West Indies. Finished goods went from Britain to Africa, slaves went from Africa to the Americas and West Indies, and tropical goods – primarily sugar but also occasionally fresh pineapples and certainly preserved ones – went from the West Indies to Britain. However, subsumed in this was another flow of trade, which saw direct commerce between the American colonies and the West Indies.

Traditional pineapple Christmas wreath in a style popularized in Colonial Williamsburg. This wreath uses flowers instead of fruit.

A timeless symbol of luxury, wealth, elegance and hospitality, pineapple was served at the society wedding of Jacqueline Bouvier and John Fitzgerald Kennedy in 1953.

Fresh pineapples came to colonial markets via this route, reaching America in a better state than those that crossed the Atlantic, keeping the pineapple in the colonial eye – if not yet in every hand – as the ultimate fruit of desire.

During the American Revolution the pineapple was cast in a new and unexpected symbolic role. As the 'Fruit of Kings', it had developed many royalist associations, from the kings, queens and courtiers who had been its patrons to the way its leaves were compared to a crown and its manner of propagating through 'heirs' to the laws of kingly succession. Yet during the American Revolution, to the rebellious colonials this most royal of fruits became a symbol of New World independence. In *The Beauties of Santa Cruz* Philip Freneau, the leading poet of the American Revolution, wrote of

The prince of fruits, whom some *jayama* call
Anana some, the happy flavoured pine;
In which unites the tastes and the juice all
Of apple, quince, peach, grape and nectarine.

Grows to perfection here, and spreads his crest
His diadem towards the parent sun
His diadem, in fiery blossoms drest,
Stands armed with swords, from potent Nature won.[25]

The pineapple
in American
colonial
architecture.
Doorway
pediment
surmounted
by a pineapple,
probably Salem,
Massachusetts.

Here the pineapple – the title 'king' replaced by that of 'prince' – is presented as the embodiment of all that was desirable in the New World, superior to Old World fruits, the natural entitlement of the victors who now controlled the new nation, protecting themselves with arms as the pineapple protected itself with its sharp leaves.

The decorative use of pineapple motifs increased, as did the demand for the fruit. After the Revolution, Washington was among the many wealthy American citizens who attempted to grow hothouse pineapples in the British fashion. A pinerie was constructed at his home at Mount Vernon and there Washington watched over the progress of his fruits, just as in Britain George III was surveying his own in the pineries at Kew Gardens and Kensington Palace. In France, the French Revolution had extinguished the aristocratic cultivation of the pineapple. French royal interest would resume with the Bourbon restoration, but before then, pineapples were reinstated by Napoleon's first consort, the Empress Josephine, who was brought up on a Martinique sugar plantation and built a grand heated pinery at her chateau, Malmaison. So, for a moment in time, monarch, empress and president – separated by politics and an ocean – were united in their passion for pineapples.

Postcard of a pineapple in a decorative wall hanging, early 20th century.

3
Queen Pine

In Britain, the pineapple continued to exert its fascination, the poet Charles Lamb (1775–1834) declaring his passion in unblushing prose:

> Pineapple is great. She is almost too transcendent – a delight if not sinful, yet so like sinning that really a tender conscienced person would do well to pause – too ravishing for mortal taste, she woundeth and excoriateth the lips that approach her – like lovers' kisses she biteth – she is a pleasure bordering on pain, from the fierceness and insanity of her relish.[1]

The pineapple was undergoing a shift in gender, seductive femininity taking over from the initial masculine imagery. By the time Queen Victoria came to the throne, the pineapple was increasingly called the 'Queen of Fruits', rather than the king.

Despite the high cost of the fruit, demand and desire had established hothouse-pineapple culture as a paying industry, facilitated by technological improvements, cheaper glass and refined horticultural techniques. Large-scale pineapple-hothouse operations were opened by nurserymen turned entrepreneur.

Once they would have catered only to the aristocracy and gentry, but now they served the rising middle classes whose emergence was a feature of the Victorian age (1837–1901). Industrialization was another distinctive feature of the Victorian period – as was a belief in scientific progress for the benefit of all. This manifested itself in developments in manufacturing and transportation, both of which would transform the fortunes of the pineapple. While shipping times under sail had steadily decreased, it was the invention of the steamship in the early nineteenth century that enabled the bulk importation of pineapples, opening a mass commercial market for them and leading to the rise of pineapple plantations.

The early Caribbean sugar planters had made fortunes, but the markets turned volatile and sugar prices dropped, exposing the problems of monoculture, especially on small islands. An additional factor was that, with the abolition of slavery, the large labour pool needed for sugar was no longer available. As *The Times* of London put it, 'there was a great aversion to the cultivation of the cane, as reminding them

Spode pineapple stand intended for displaying a pineapple, *c.* 1820, bone china painted in green and gilded. The receptacle in the centre is for the fruit's stalk.

of their slavery.'[2] This, along with the slump in sugar prices and demand, drove the search for a new cash crop and pineapple presented itself. Pineapple, as the London *Morning Post* pointed out, was 'hardy, remarkably easy of propagation, requiring a small amount of labour and capital; in short a modicum of desultory labour will suffice'.[3] This, coinciding with the emergence of steamship transportation, set off a tropical scramble to establish pineapple plantations, farms and smallholdings.

The main types of pineapple cultivated commercially today are Gold MD-2, Smooth Cayenne, Spanish Red and Queen, but the names and varieties grown in 1847 give insight into lost diversity and a vanished world of far-flung colonial plantations. Among them were the Black Antigua, remarkably juicy and highly flavoured; the Blood Red from Jamaica, a reddish-chocolate colour when ripe; the Demerara, white and firm; the Green Java, juicy and melting, a plant first obtained by Sir Stamford Raffles during his residence in Java; the Lemon Queen from Barbados; the St Vincent's Green; the Cape Coast from Africa; the Otaheite from the South Pacific; the Bahama Sugarloaf; the Surinam Striped; the Scarlet Brazilian; the Trinidad; the Sumatra and many, many more in a range of sizes and shapes, including conical and pyramidal.[4]

Soon large shipments of pineapple from the West Indies were being unloaded on docks in Britain and along the American East Coast, and jostling home-grown hothouse pineapples in the markets and shops. In the heyday of the pineries, commentators had noted that

> the pineapple unites the taste and flavour of many exquisite fruits; but alas! It grows only in the rich soil of hothouses and graces only the tables of the great. The common apple has but one taste to boast, but our

orchards produce it in plenty and its plenty is useful to the high and to the low.[5]

The comparison between the apple and pineapple would often be made – the apple was cast as 'honest' and 'upright', thoroughly British or American as the case might be, while the pineapple was portrayed as foreign, exotic, seductive and dangerous. Now, for the first time, the pineapple was within the reach of all.

Newly arrived pineapples were auctioned at the docks or in the wholesale fruit markets, of which the largest in England was London's Covent Garden where they made a fine sight, piled up on the pavements for people to come and marvel at. The best fruits found their way to the high-class fruiterers and provisioners who served the aristocracy and gentry – at least those who were not provided for by the produce of their own country estates and pineries. Due to the different types of pineapple available, and points of origin, there were great differences in the quality of the imported fruit. The quickest steamship transit from the West Indies might take three weeks to reach Britain, but it often took longer. The fruit did not arrive at the ports from the pineapple fields quickly or easily, especially in the early days of the trade, and once there spent a lot of time sitting in the heat while consignments were put together. As a result, many pineapples still spoiled on their way across the Atlantic, while some travelled better than others. Queen pineapples had the best flavour, but they were more delicate and therefore more difficult to transport without damage than other varieties. So, for the elite, it was still possible to speak of the 'superior quality, the more delicate appearance, the exquisite fragrance and flavour which distinguish the English from the imported fruit'.[6] However, these prime home-grown pineapples would never have been widely available.

The ordinary imported pineapples were bought by the merchants who catered to the rising 'people of the middling sort'. In Britain, the Victorian period was a time of unparalleled social mobility. Industrialization created new wealth and opportunities, and a new social class with money and aspirations. Social life became a minefield, with the new rich and those slightly below them under tremendous pressure to avoid showing by thought, word or deed that they were not 'one of us', that is, established members of the elite. For those new to polite society, formal dining was regarded as a particular ordeal. Correct table manners, the 'right' menus and 'correct' ways of serving and eating became a middle-class preoccupation, fuelled by the publication of many new books on etiquette, household management and cookery. This literature of gentrification and self-improvement was also a literature of fantasy. It depicted a highly idealized upper-class world in which few people lived and behaved exactly as described on an everyday basis, and it was a world to which very few of the readers would actually ever gain entry. It was, however, considered vitally important to know how the upper class lived, and to imitate it as far as possible. These were new social fields for the imported pineapple to conquer – and it did.

Pineapples now made their debut on an ever-wider circle of dinner tables, to the disapproval of those who considered themselves superior. As one of these people observed,

> although a noble pine is an ornament to any table, it becomes rather commonplace when it is seen too often and I have heard of one going the round of a series of west-end dinner parties for some weeks. It might have been used in the same way longer, and been equally useful, if it had been made of wax or cast-iron.[7]

The imported pineapples also provided new opportunities for social subterfuge. The *Pall Mall Gazette* warned that

> A curious practice has of late been adopted by fruiterers
> which cannot be called adulteration but is very near
> akin to it. Persons on buying West Indian pineapples
> at fruiterers' shops are asked whether they wish to
> purchase 'heads' to the fruit. In other words, West Indian
> pineapples are dressed for dessert at a small cost as
> British hothouse pines by the ingenious plan of insert-
> ing in the summit of the fruit a tuft or crown of leaves
> belonging to the later, and thus guests are deceived into
> the notion that the pineapple which graces the table was
> grown in the hothouse of their host, who probably
> never had a hothouse, and knows nothing about the cul-
> tivation of pines . . . A West India pineapple has no more
> right to wear a British crown than an apple or a peach

Dinner table with pineapple, from *Mrs Beeton's Book of Household Management* (1901 edition).

'Dessert', from *Mrs Beeton's Book of Household Management* (1901 edition).

has to employ rouge for the purpose of concealing its pallor or heightening its bloom.[8]

The most remarkable document in the Victorian literature of domestic, social and culinary self-improvement was *Mrs Beeton's Book of Household Management,* an encyclopaedic work that both reflected and perpetuated the aspirations to gentrification of the new middle class. There were many other books, but this one was the largest and most comprehensive. It was also the most influential, stretching to several editions over many years, and it gives insight into the social progress of the pineapple.

Victorian lace flounce with a pineapple pattern, *c.* 1860s.

The elite way of eating pineapple at the dessert course was to cut it into slices and serve it without further embellishment, so that diners could enjoy the full savour of the fruit brought to ripeness at great effort and expense. It was a testament to the excellence of the pineapple that neither sugar nor liqueur was needed to enhance it. In the coloured illustrations that are a delight of the Beeton book, the 'dessert' page shows fine cherries, raspberries, plums, mulberries and peaches arranged in dessert dishes, and a whole golden pineapple complete with crown in the place of honour on a fruit stand. This was a vision of *comme il faut*, how things were done in grand homes. However, the pineapple recipes reveal a different truth. In middle-class homes, the fruit invariably ended up as preserved pineapple (pineapple in sugar syrup), pineapple chips (sugared pine dried in a very low oven) and pineapple fritters in which a West Indian pineapple was sliced thinly, soaked in brandy or liqueur and sugar for four hours, then dipped into batter and deep fried, before being served up hot and sprinkled with sugar on a white doily. Other publications offered recipes for pineapple pies, puddings, fritters and dumplings, which often began with instructions for grating a peeled pineapple – a truly ripe pineapple would fall apart at the very mention of a grater. With grating and so much sugar involved in the preparation, the hardness and sourness of many of the imported pineapples can easily be imagined.

Apart from removing the sourness, there was another practical reason to preserve pineapple with sugar. In the hot-houses the aim was to start off seedlings at different times to ensure a supply of fresh pineapple throughout the year, but the natural outdoor pineapples of the West Indies were seasonal. They ripened in July and August, when there was likely to be a glut in the market, with fruit plentiful and cheap, after which they disappeared until the next season. Indeed, all non-hothouse fruit was seasonal, which is why there was a great call for preserved fruit and for natural and imitation fruit essences that could be used to flavour desserts and confectionery out of season, pineapple essence being especially popular. In addition, sugar had changed the Euro-American palate and many people now preferred fruits of all kinds sugared, even those that did not require sweetening.

This did not meet with universal approval. In the weekly magazine *All the Year Round*, owned and edited by Charles Dickens, an article entitled 'Confectioner's Botany', which Dickens – who took a close interest in food and drink – may well have written, railed at artificial flavourings and over-sugared fruit. Pineapple oil or essence, it revealed, was composed of butyric acid mixed with ethyl or ether. Was anything, the writer wondered, really what it professed to be? A visit to London's Fortnum & Mason – 'that tempting emporium of all that is elegant, tasteful and delicious in the art of confectionary' – disclosed displays of 'genuine botanical specimens, so disguised and sweetened with candied sugar that the eye would never detect portions of some of our commonest wild flowers' or uncommon fruits.[9] Today Fortnum & Mason still offers candied violets, rose petals and angelica, along with a fine selection of glacé fruits including pineapple slices and, occasionally, rare and splendid candied whole small pineapples, complete with their crowns.

As a result of domestic improvements, including the invention of a wide range of hand-cranked freezers, ice cream was now for commoners as well as for kings, and pineapple ice was a great favourite. There are many recipes for pineapple ice creams and water ices, often frozen in fancy pineapple-shaped moulds and presented with a great flourish. Mrs A. B. Marshall, a specialist in fancy ices who also ran Marshall's School of Cookery in London, advised that for 'Versailles Pineapple Cream' the leaves of the mould should be filled with green pistachio ice cream, and the body with pineapple ice to which had been added the pulp and very finely chopped peel of six tangerines, to give colour.[10]

The least choice of the imported pineapples found their way to people who were not concerned with confectionery and flavourings, but just wanted to taste the pineapple 'for the fun of the thing'. The poor did not usually patronize shops; they bought their fruit off street barrows from costermongers (fruit and vegetable sellers), and the arrival of West Indian pineapples was recorded by social researcher and journalist Henry Mayhew, whose prose captures Victorian London's vibrant street culture:

Pineapples, when they were first introduced, were a rich harvest to the costermonger. They made more money 'working' these than any other article. They cost them about 4 pence each, one with the other, good and bad together, and were sold by the costermonger at from 12 pence to 18 pence. The public were not aware then that

FANCY ICE MOULDS IN PEWTER.

No. 42.—DUCK.   **No. 43.—SWAN.**

1 quart, £1. 3*s*. 0*d*.   2 pints, £1. 1*s*. 0*d*.

| No. 44. | No. 45. | No. 46. |
| DOVE. | BUNCH OF GRAPES. | CAULIFLOWER. |

1¼ pints, 16*s*. 0*d*.   1 quart, £1. 5*s*. 0*d*.   1 quart, £1. 5*s*. 0*d*.

No. 47.—HEN.   **No. 48.—FISH.**

1 quart, £1. 1*s*. 0*d*.   1 quart, £1. 1*s*. 0*d*.

| No. 49. | No. 50. | No. 51. |
| PINEAPPLE. | BASKET OF FLOWERS. | BUNCH OF ASPARAGUS. |

1 quart, 20*s*. 0*d*.   1 quart, £1. 5*s*. 0*d*.   1 quart & ½ pint, £1. 5*s*. 0*d*.

SPECIMEN PAGE FROM 'BOOK OF MOULDS.'

Fancy ice cream moulds from Mrs A. B. Marshall's *Fancy Ices* (1894).

the pines they sold were 'salt-water touched,' and the people bought them as fast as they could sell, not only by the whole one, but at 1 penny a slice – for those who could not afford to give 12 pence would have a slice as a taste for 1 penny. They were a novelty when they first came up. The costermongers used to have flags flying at the head of their barrows, and gentlefolks used to stop them in the street; indeed, the sale for them was chiefly among 'the gentry.' The poorer people – sweeps, dustmen, cab-men – used to have pennyworths, but gentlepeople used to buy a whole one to take home, so that all the family might have a taste. This was four years ago, but since then there has not been such a call for them. The vessel in which they first came over was exposed to very bad weather, and the salt-water damaged them so as to make them un-saleable by the regular fruiterer. They were bought cheap by the costermonger, and he made a great deal of money out of them.[11]

For a penny, the poor could taste paradise, and from then on pineapple slices or penny chunks handed out on the end of a fork were a favoured treat of the working poor. However, all was not well for the pineapple, which now became a victim of the Victorian paradox of progress.

The aim of scientific and economic progress was the betterment and improvement of the human condition, but any gains challenged established social hierarchies. As trans-portation, education and mass-production began to transform everyday life, would people still 'know their place' and be content to keep it? The elite felt threatened by the new middle class, which in turn felt threatened by the rising work-ing poor. Beyond mere snobbery and a desire to maintain one's own position there was a concern that the loss of social

Transfer-printed plate with a 'Buah Nanas' pineapple pattern produced by J. & M. P. Bell Ltd, Glasgow, c. 1888.

distinctions could result in political instability at a time when Europe was emerging from a long period of unrest.

When elite goods became available to all through scientific and technological progress, they were transformed into dangerous commodities that blurred the class boundaries. The pineapple was the epitome of this kind of elite goods. Just as the elite had disapproved of the appearance of pineapples on middle-class tables, so the middle classes resented having to share the fruit with the poor, complaining in the press that

> The street markets of London offer some curious contradictions in values at the present time. What used to be regarded as luxury fruit is now to be found at very moderate prices on the stalls and on some of the barrows which go through the great thoroughfares.[12]

In satirical prints, 'inappropriate' people eating pineapples – exactly who they were depended on one's point of view –

became a metaphor for the ills of progress, rather than its benefits. The pineapple began to lose its social cachet, a process that was now accelerated by another progressive invention, namely canning.

Canning was a French technique that became public in 1809, and originally involved glass jars rather than the metal tins which soon followed. The instigation was military, with Napoleon offering a reward of 12,000 francs for an effective and cheap way of preserving food to feed the French army. In Britain, the first use of canning was also military, for rations for the British army and navy, but as the process was refined it was adapted for general commercial use, with pineapple canneries established in the West Indies in the 1880s.

Pineapple canning overcame the two persistent problems of seasonality and distance. Now fruit could be left to grow fully ripe, canned at or near the point of origin, then transported over long distances without risk of spoilage, to be available to the consumer all through the year. In his journal of the voyage of the *Beagle*, Charles Darwin had written that in Tahiti pineapples were so abundant and the islands so oversupplied that the fruits were treated 'in the same wasteful manner as we would eat turnips'. Now the pineapples that had languished in the faraway colonies for lack of sufficiently speedy shipping could, in cans, find a market in Britain and other parts of the Empire – and although pineapple was canned in light syrup, it was not as heavily sugared as *confitures* or preserves.

Canning was not universally popular in England – some decried the growing dependence on imported food in a nation that had until recently been proudly self-sufficient, while others feared the contamination and poisoning that happened in the early days of the process, and as always new opportunities for subterfuge presented themselves. A letter to *The Times* warned:

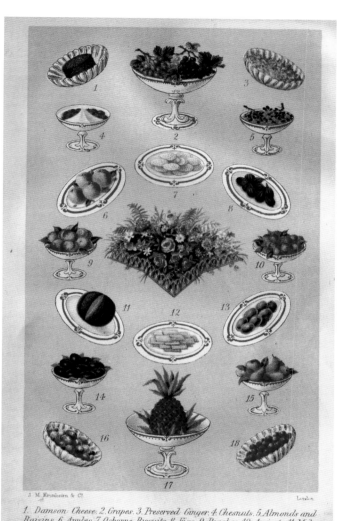

1. Damson Cheese. 2. Grapes. 3. Preserved Ginger. 4. Chesnuts. 5. Almonds and Raisins. 6. Apples. 7. Osborne Biscuits. 8. Figs. 9. Peaches. 10. Apricots. 11. Melon. 12. Lemon Wafers. 13. Greengages. 14. Plums. 15. Pears. 16. Crystalised Fruit. 17. Pine Apple. 18. Crystalised Cherries.

A less formal dessert presentation, from *Warnes Model Cookery and Housekeeping Book* (1893 edition).

In recent years a large trade has been developed of repacking into glass fruits which have originally been imported into this country in tins. I refer particularly to pineapple, apricots, peaches and pears . . . The method has arisen in consequence of a prejudice which exists amongst a large proportion of well-to-do people, who expect when they buy these goods in glass they are avoiding all possibility of metallic contact . . . at present a great fraud is being perpetrated on the public, because they are paying twice the price for this food through the deception . . . 75 per cent of the fruit . . . which are exposed for sale in London in glass bottles have been originally packed in tins.[13]

While taste and contamination were no doubt a concern, a main factor was maintaining class distinctions. Elite prejudice against canning was strong. The undeniable benefits and convenience of preserved fruit might now be available to all, but it was important that there be a superior as well as an ordinary way of delivering the goods. It was certainly the case that canning was gradually transforming the larders of the middle classes and the working poor, and once again, 'progress' was perceived in a negative way, with critics decrying the 'piles of gaudy canisters that embalm every constituent of a dinner, from the soup to the pineapple',[14] which too easily tempted the public. They also deplored the way that village shops and humble provisioners in town:

seem to be stocked not with necessities but with luxuries . . . with salmon and pineapple more easily procurable than fresh meat or even wholesome bread, it is hardly surprising that many village housekeepers . . . lay out the weekly wage on forms of diet that would have scandalized their grandmothers.[15]

The pineapple as everyday art: crocheted doily with a pineapple pattern.

However, there was no putting the genie back in the bottle or the can. In Britain, pineapple was now established as an edible oxymoron – a truly everyday luxury.

In America as in Britain, private pineries had now been largely abandoned as uneconomic extravagances. Shipments of fresh and canned pineapple came in from the West Indies, but the nation had expanded across the North American continent and these imported Caribbean products were insufficient to satisfy demand on the West Coast. In some quarters the pineapple's old associations with luxury and the exotic continued to draw disapproval, particularly among the puritan element on the East Coast. As the New England author, philosopher and naturalist Henry Thoreau wrote:

> The bitter sweet of a white oak acorn which you nibble
> in a bleak November walk over the tawny earth is more

to me than a slice of imported pineapple. We do not think much of table fruits. They are especially for aldermen and epicures. They do not feed the imagination.[16]

Soon, however, the pineapple would become accessible to all in America, and would feed – indeed fire – the popular imagination worldwide in an unprecedented and unimagined way.

4
Hawaiian Pineapple

When, in 1778, Captain James Cook sailed across the Pacific through the eye of the old Manila Galleon route, he 'discovered' a paradise – the islands of Hawaii. Here, between the deep sea and green valleys bridged by rainbows, the pineapple would find its perfect home. In economic terms, the later history of these islands paralleled that of the Caribbean – a need to produce income met first by sugar, then by the pineapple. However, the sequence took place later in time, and in very different social and political circumstances.

At the time of Cook's arrival, the Hawaiians were involved in wars of conquest leading towards the creation of a single paramount kingship over all the islands. Accelerated by the introduction of Western arms and influence, the process was completed by 1810, and absolute monarchy on a European model was established under the rule of the first king, Kamehameha I (*c*. 1758–1819).

Hawaii's strategic position in mid-ocean opened up transpacific trade, and the new kingdom soon grew rich on supplying the whaling industry and supporting the trade routes that linked the West Coast of North America with China. Trade attracted foreign residents – British, French, American and others. The last-named included an advisor to Kamehameha I,

Rainbow over pineapple field, Oahu, Hawaii.

the Spaniard Don Francisco de Paula Marin, a keen horticulturist who was responsible for the first known introduction of pineapples to Hawaii, growing them in his garden. Among the Americans were Congregationalist missionaries from New England who arrived uninvited in 1820.

When whaling and the China trade fell off at the end of the 1850s, sugar became the new cash crop. Plantations were established, more foreigners flocked to the islands to make their fortunes, and the islands became renowned for their high colonial culture, a whirl of dances, parties and gracious dinners in the European style. Under royal patronage traditional Hawaiian practices – of which the missionaries disapproved – also continued, notably hula dancing and the great feasts known as *luaus*, with the lavish *luaus* given by the royal family in which guests feasted on *kalua* baked pork becoming legendary.[1] There were echoes of high society in the Caribbean, with one significant difference – Hawaii was not a colony, but a sovereign kingdom. However, it was a kingdom increasingly threatened from within and without.

Within the kingdom, the early missionaries had eroded the absolute power of the monarchy, and their descendants along with the increasing numbers of new American residents wished to take political control of the islands in order to run the sugar industry, over which the ruler still had ultimate authority. The threat from without came from America, which provided the market for Hawaiian sugar. As the nineteenth century drew to a close, America – almost alone among the major powers – was a nation without an empire, or a post-empire. Elsewhere in the world, the nineteenth century was a time of scrambling for colonies, with the great powers snapping up unclaimed territories, often in the tropics, now viable propositions due to improved transportation and technology.

Preoccupied with domestic matters – the westward expansion across the North American continent and the Civil War (1861–5) – America found itself with no foreign possessions and, especially, no land in the tropics, and therefore no tropical products. There were attempts to grow sugar in Louisiana and pineapples in Florida, but neither flourished sufficiently to supply the nation's needs. Hawaii lay on America's western doorstep. American advisors had already noted the islands' strategic position – the United States and the Kingdom of Hawaii were on a collision course. The fatal blow came on 17 January 1893, when an American-backed group overthrew Hawaii's ruler, Queen Liliuokalani (1838–1917), imprisoned her in the Iolani Palace and established an interim government before formal annexation to the United States in 1898.

With Hawaii now an American colony in all but name and Hawaiian sugar no longer subject to punitive American import taxes, the industry flourished and the new government set out to 'Americanize' Hawaii, drawing a veil over traditional

Pineapple landmark. For many years this water tower in the shape of a pineapple – 'the largest pineapple in the world' – dominated the Honolulu cannery site of the Hawaiian Pineapple Company, later Dole Pineapple.

Hawaiian culture, which did not figure in the new official version of the islands' attractions. In 1924 a *National Geographic Magazine* feature described the islands as 'America's Strongest Outpost of Defense – The Volcanic and Floral Wonderland of the World',[2] and Honolulu as having miles of concrete roads, daily quotations from the New York stock market and a fine country club with a golf course.

Along with other agricultural crops, the pineapple had been commercially planted on a small scale to supply elite Hawaiian tables, passing ships and the Californian market grown wealthy from the Gold Rush, but these early efforts had not prospered, a major export problem being that the ripe fruits quickly glutted the West Coast markets and there was no way of getting them to the East Coast still fresh. As one commentator observed of the early period:

> The history of the Hawaiian pineapple reads like a
> romance in which a number of heroes struggled with
> the unknown forces of inanimate nature and the better-
> known vagaries of insect and human nature, and finally
> won the victory. It was a short, sharp fight.[3]

The winner was James Dole, who in 1900 established the
Hawaiian Pineapple Company and a large plantation on the
main island of Oahu. His efforts received little encouragement, but he opened a cannery and began to export canned
pineapple to America. With sugar prices proving volatile,
Dole soon had imitators and competitors, the best known
being the California Packing Company or CPC (Del Monte)
and Libby McNeil & Libby, along with smaller local pineapple producers.

In Hawaii, the pineapple found ideal growing conditions
– a natural hothouse where the fruits could ripen to perfection
out of doors. With the problems of seasonality and transportation overcome by canning, the challenge now was to expand
the market. Canning was still relatively new and distrust and
prejudice were widespread, something all canners had to
overcome. Like other fruit canners, the Hawaiian pineapple
producers initially emphasized the general benefits of year-
found availability, hygiene and convenience, beginning advertising in 1909. 'Sun-ripened on the field, not picked green
and ripened afterwards',[4] said one advertisement. 'Picked
Ripe – Canned Right – The full flavour, quality and tenderness
of ripeness',[5] began another, with an illustration showing a
worker, muffled and hatted against the sun, bent double in
a pineapple field, tending to the fruit. Other advertisements
showed how the Ginaca machine, invented for Dole cannery
by Henry Gabriel Ginaca and which revolutionized pineapple
canning, peeled and cored pineapples.

Workers in Hawaiian pineapple fields, *c.* 1910–25.

When the images of factory machinery and field labourers failed to arouse the enthusiasm of the American housewife, the pineapple canners turned to a more practical domestic approach. Recipes – free or at a nominal cost – were an established way of promoting the use of food products. Often

devised by noted culinary writers of the day or gathered from the public in the course of well-publicized competitions, the brochures, booklets and recipes that appeared in women's magazines and on the women's pages in newspapers were highly valued by readers, and were generally more popular, influential and reflective of changing culinary tastes than cookbooks.

In order to be commercially successful in the mass market, producers had to insinuate their products into the mainstream food culture of early twentieth-century America. The regional and ethnic cuisines that distinguish American cuisine today were not allowed to feature on the official national food map of the period. 'American' food – consolidating in its uniformity and ubiquity – consisted of a meat-potatoes-and-plain-vanilla cuisine, heartily democratic and harking back to New England foodways from which many of the early cookery experts sprung. In 1914 the Hawaiian Pineapple Packers Association brought out a booklet entitled *How We Serve Hawaiian Canned Pineapple*. It contained pictures of labourers, gave a rhapsodic account of pineapple fields and described the canning process, but then went on to present pineapple recipes from such luminary 'authorities on cooking' as Fannie Merritt Farmer, author of *The Boston Cooking-School Cookbook* (Pineapple Compote) and Sarah Tyson Rorer, founder of the Philadelphia School of Cookery (Pineapple Jelly). Pineapple jelly made with canned fruit was a great novelty as the enzymes in fresh pineapple had prevented gelatin from setting (see recipe for gelatin salad, p. 134).

In the 1914 booklet, all the recipes were for pineapple desserts or fruit salads of some kind, but by 1925, when the Association of Hawaiian Pineapple Canners brought out a new edition with some additional recipes under the title *Ninety-Nine Tempting Pineapple Treats,* two non-dessert recipes had been included – a ham baked with pineapple, and a pineapple stuffing for fish. The Association of Hawaiian Pineapple Canners then ran a large national competition for pineapple recipes, publishing the best of them in 1926 as *Hawaiian Pineapple as 100 Good Cooks Serve It.*

This booklet reveals the extent to which pineapple was beginning to infiltrate the meat and vegetable parts of the

Jellied salads that mixed canned pineapple and other fruit with fresh vegetables were a great novelty.

American menu. Along with the usual battery of desserts and salads were recipes for pineapple meat loaf; pineapple poultry stuffing for duck, guinea hen or turkey; pineapple Welsh Rarebit and even Boston Baked Beans with pineapple (see recipe, p. 135). In 1927, Dole's Hawaiian Pineapple Company brought out the booklet *The Kingdom That Grew Out of a Little Boy's Garden*, which combined a brief company history with 'thirty new and delightful ways to serve Hawaiian Pineapple'. *Good Housekeeping* magazine provided ten recipes for 'glorious salads', *Pictorial Review* contributed 'ten of the most delicious desserts you have ever known – desserts that will make your dinners long remembered', and *McCall's* magazine furnished 'ten wonderful main course dishes' such as Planked Steak with Pineapple Border and Pineapple-stuffed Tomatoes. The canned pineapple was now established on the nation's tables; utterly conventional and as all-American as apples or pears – from which, in many of the recipes, it was virtually indistinguishable. Then everything changed.

While canned pineapple exports were making steady progress, world sugar prices collapsed and the fledgling Hawaiian tourist industry floundered. Tourists had little interest in the official version of Hawaii as transplanted American suburbia and stayed away in droves, for the attraction of Hawaii, then as now, was the exotic and the strange, albeit in a safe setting. In order to save tourism in this time of economic need, it was necessary to reverse the work of the previous decades, and 're-Hawaiianize' the islands for the benefit of visitors, creating a romanticized version of the past that owed more to Hollywood than to history.

The few grass houses that had not been torn down were renovated and displayed as tourist attractions, while hula

Pineapple upside-down cake, the iconic canned fruit dessert.

dancing – which had long been forbidden in public – was now revived in modified melodic form. The 'natives', previously invisible, were recast as players in the pageant of a reinvented traditional Hawaii. Glossing over the inconvenient truth of the overthrow of the monarchy and, before that, the fierce aristocratic warrior society that Cook had encountered, 'Old Hawaii' was portrayed as a democratic paradise where chiefs and subjects consorted happily together in perpetual singing, dancing and feasting, and the *luau* – long discouraged by the missionaries – now became a highlight of the new Hawaiian tourist experience. With this dramatic transformation, Hawaii became the ultimate holiday destination of desire, with the pineapple as its culinary symbol.

The only way to reach the islands in those days was by luxury liner from the American West Coast, a four and a half day cruise on a white ship of the Matson Navigation Company. These crossings – renowned for their romance, elegance and service – were a seductive introduction to the reinvented Hawaii. In this, the specially commissioned covers for the menus, marvellous examples of high tourist art, played a key part. Highly collectible from the outset, there was a different one for every night of the cruise. A splendid menu cover by Eugene Savage – *Island Feast* – showed a Hawaiian chief surrounded by beautiful maidens, seated at a feast of roast pig and pineapple. This *luau* could never have taken place in Old Hawaii. In the old days, taboos forbade men and women to eat together, chiefs did not eat with commoners, women were not allowed to eat pork and pineapples were unknown on the islands. Nonetheless, this vision of polite primitivism took root in the popular imagination. Roast pig was not very aesthetic, but the pineapple – drawing on its history – re-emerged as the embodiment of the tropics and the exotic.

When visitors arrived at the elegant new beachside hotels in Waikiki, this was the sort of scene they expected to encounter – and did. *Luaus* were held in the hotel gardens, the food served on tables decorated with pineapples. The entertainment consisted of singing and hula dancing, often performed by ladies in sarongs, a garment that was invented by the designer Edith Head of Paramount Studios for Dorothy Lamour to wear in the film *Jungle Princess*.

As America and the world fell in love with exotic Hawaii, the pineapple canners realized that here was a new commercial opportunity. Initially, their appeal was one of vicarious travel, beginning in this advertisement from 1924 with:

> And if you can't visit Hawaii this year – at least plan to enjoy, at home, the never-to-be-forgotten flavour of Hawaii's favourite fruit! Serve canned Hawaiian Pine-apple often – all year round – the *Sliced* as a dessert and salad fruit just as it comes from the can – the *Crushed* in pies, cakes, salads, sundaes, fruit-cocktails, and in a host of other tempting made-up dishes.[6]

It went on to give recipes for pineapple sundae, pineapple meringue pie and pineapple fruit cup.

Soon the Hawaii pineapple producers and the tourist industry threw caution to the tradewinds, as the island experience grew ever more enthusiastically exotic. There were several reasons for this. Travel became less expensive and exclusive, especially after aircraft ushered in the age of mass tourism. Hollywood fell in love with Hawaii, using it as a location for films such as *Bird of Paradise*, *Waikiki Wedding*, *Hawaii Calls*, *Hawaiian Nights* and the Charlie Chan mysteries. The Second World War had acquainted a generation of servicemen with the Far East, and the island population itself was becoming

more cosmopolitan. Chinese and Japanese workers had been brought in to work the sugar and pineapple fields in the nineteenth century. By 1924, the Japanese made up 40 per cent of the island populace and were increasing – and intermarriage was producing a mixed population and increasingly complex cuisine known in the islands as 'hapa-haole'.

Closely allied to this cosmopolitanism was the food, drink and decorative style called 'tiki', associated with Victor Bergeron of Trader Vic's restaurants. His was a lush and swashbuckling approach to cookery, evoking faraway islands, long drinks and nights too short for all the fun and good island food that was

97

Cosmopolitan *luau*: island '*luau* plate lunch' showing traditional roast kalua-style pig with chicken teriyaki, rice and pineapple.

to be had. Among the signature Trader Vic dishes were Bongo Bongo soup (oyster velouté with spinach) and pineapple duck. All of these influences were reflected in the *luau,* which now offered Chinese, Japanese and utterly fanciful foods in addition to the traditional Hawaiian roast *kalua* pork, sweet potatoes and *haupia* coconut pudding.

Sliced fresh pineapple was promoted and served on the islands. Elsewhere, instead of selling pineapple for conventional dishes, pineapple producers now leaped on the *luau* bandwagon, promoting pineapple, *luau* cookery and Hawaii as a gastronomic trinity so successfully that, worldwide, any dish described as 'Hawaiian' is still assumed to contain pineapple.

After attending a *luau* on the islands – either in body or in the imagination – it was thought that people would want to recreate the experience at home, which gave rise to a wave of *luau* cookbooks and party guides. Conventional dishes were now abandoned – instead there were recipes for Pineapple

Beef Kabobs, Polynesian Meat Balls, Pineapple Pork Waikiki and much more. The Dole Company brought out *A Hawaiian Luau,* which began:

> The growing popularity of Hawaiian parties prompted us to assemble some ideas and recipes used on the 'mainland' to create the wonderfully relaxed atmosphere of a *luau.*[7]

Competitors Del Monte brought out their own *luau* cookbook, which stated: 'Create a ray of Hawaiian sunshine for your table with Del Monte Pineapple',[8] and contained recipes for two iconic dishes of the 1950s through to the 1970s – pineapple spare ribs and pineapple upside-down cake. Whether canned or fresh, to buy and eat a Hawaiian pineapple was to consume a dream of paradise.

The classic tourist *luau* offerings: roast pig and pineapple.

The famous — and infamous — 'Hawaiian' ham and pineapple pizza.

Sometimes it was about another kind of dream. One of the stranger episodes in the history of the pineapple in its fresh form was its starring role in the 1980s Beverly Hills Diet, popularly known as the 'Pineapple Diet', which was celebrated in one of the best-selling diet books of the century. Devised by Judy Mazel, 'diet guru' to the Hollywood stars, it mixed the idea of food combining with the properties of selected foods — notably pineapple — that are rich in enzymes which, the theory goes, burn up fat. The answer to the age-old question of 'how to be as thin as you like for the rest of your life' was, apparently, to eat a lot of fresh pineapple. The diet was refined and tested by Mazel on the islands, surrounded by supplies of prime Hawaiian pineapples. Whatever the effect of the diet on the human figure, it certainly did a lot for the sales figures of Hawaiian pineapples.

Pineapples sprouted on the colourful Hawaiian shirts and *muumuus* worn on the islands by visitors and residents alike. There were 'pineapple patterns' on the famous Hawaiian appliqué quilts, pineapple-print upholstery fabrics for curtains and the deep lounging couches popular on the islands and framed pineapple prints for walls, one favourite being by the artist Georgia O'Keeffe. Carved items in *koa* wood were a popular form of local tourist art, and pineapples appeared as bowls and platters in the shapes of half-pineapples, and as finials on salad servers. There were china services decorated with pineapples, pineapple jewellery, pineapple coffee mugs, pineapple ice buckets, pineapple salt-and-pepper shakers and ceramic pineapples for tiki cocktails. Periodically, there would be attempts to use pineapple fibres to make cloth – one popular version was known as 'pineapple tweed'.

Pineapple was not just for tourists. Islanders developed their own pineapple cuisine, two distinctive dishes being the

A local favourite: Hawaiian pineapple with white rice and sweet-and-sour Vienna sausage.

ever-popular pineapple spare ribs and sweet-and-sour dishes using Spam and Vienna sausage. It is a little-known fact that Hawaii has the world's largest per capita consumption of Spam, with Vienna sausage not far behind.

Pineapple had another life far from the tourist beaches and *luaus* of Waikiki. It was one of the foundations of the economy and society of the islands, so inseparable in its heyday that the story of the Hawaiian islands *was* the story of pineapple. Canned Hawaiian pineapple was without a doubt the best in the world, partly because of the ideal growing conditions in the islands, and partly because of the care and attention lavished on it. While pineapples in the wild may have looked after themselves, commercial pineapple growing was an intensive operation. Fields were cleared and pineapple crowns were planted in rows, with the 'eye' of the fruit appearing eighteen months later. The fruits matured at 22 months and expert pickers went through the fields, testing for

The new Hawaii fusion cuisine: grilled mahimahi with pineapple salsa.

Exotic pineapple recipes were a passport to culinary adventure.

ripeness. In the 1930s the ripe fruits were picked and carried to the roadside, where other workers cut off the crowns, graded the pineapples by size and put them into crates that were then taken to the cannery by truck, train or barge.

Pineapple was grown on five of the eight main Hawaiian islands, with Lanai – the 'pineapple island' – completely given over to the fruit. June, July and August were the months of the main harvest. Pineapples from the outer islands were brought to Honolulu in barges pulled by tugboats. The long, low outlines of the pineapple barges could be glimpsed far out to sea from Waikiki Beach. Occasionally a pineapple would tumble off the barge, drift through the surfers and float shore-wards, washing up at the feet of delighted tourists.

Once the pineapples arrived in Honolulu they were taken from the docks to the nearby tin-roofed canneries in Iwilei – models of industrial efficiency – where they were peeled and cored on the Ginaca machine. They were then put onto a conveyor belt that carried them down the centre of a long table lined on either side by 'trimmers' – girls with knives who trimmed off any remaining peel. From here the fruit passed through a slicing machine, then onto a second long table lined on both sides by 'packers', girls who sorted the slices and packed them into open cans. In addition to slices, pineapple came in different grades and cuts. The filled cans were stacked in trays at the end of the packers' table, then collected by the trayboy who took the filled cans off to be sealed. All of this was accomplished in the height of summer, in great heat and noise, suffused with the sweet smell of the pineapples, intoxicating in its intensity. From here, Hawaiian canned pineapple went around the globe, making the islands for a time one of the world's largest producers of fresh pineapple, and certainly the biggest exporter of canned pineapple.

Even when mass tourism was no longer a novelty, the magic of the islands and Hawaiian pineapples never faded; it was kept alight by musicals like *South Pacific*, by James Michener's epic novel *Hawaii*, in which pineapples play a role, by television series like *Hawaii Five-O*, where pineapple fields often served as a backdrop, and by 'retro-*luaus*' and 'retro-tiki lounge' culture – except that it was not retro in Hawaii, because there it had never gone away. As the twentieth century drew to a close, the rising costs of land and labour on the islands, along with competition from foreign producers, brought the reign of the Hawaiian pineapple to a close. Today the Honolulu canneries are a heritage site and visitor destination, but small producers still grow the perfect golden fruit for island tables, local families still cook from a repertoire of pineapple dishes, pineapple stars in the new Hawaii fusion cookery and tourists still enjoy *luaus* with pineapple. In the popular imagination, the pineapple and the exotic paradise islands of Hawaii will always be as one.

5
Drinking the Pineapple

Almost as soon as Columbus realized that the pineapple could be eaten, he discovered that it could also be drunk, and that the natives seemed to prefer it as a drink. There were good reasons for this. In the tropics, when the heat and humidity overwhelmed the appetite, the Tupi and other native peoples relied on a repertoire of sustaining drinks and gruels – alcoholic and not – for nourishment, in preference to more solid foods. Columbus was struck by the diversity and ubiquity of these drinks, which he called 'wine', recording in his journal that

> They make another wine out of a fruit which was found in the island of Guadeloupe, like a great pine cone. This plant is sown in extensive fields from the sprout which grows at the top of that very pine cone . . . the plant lasts three or four years continually bearing fruit.[1]

The method in general use involved grating or crushing fruit and straining out the juice, then sometimes boiling it with water and adding flavourings, and at other times just letting it ferment. As Peter Martyr d'Anghiera reported:

A WEST INDIA SPORTSMAN.

Make haste with the Sangaree, Quashie, and tell Quaco to drive the Birds up to me ___ I'm ready

West Indies rum and planter, English satirical print, 1807.

these people eat only fruits of which they have a great variety and very different from ours. The beverages they offered were white and red wine, not made from grapes but from various kinds of crushed fruits, which were not at all disagreeable.[2]

Hans Staden, who was taken captive by the Tupi in Brazil in 1552, described drinking parties that went on for days and nights, fuelled by wine made from manioc root, bananas, palms, and *abacaxi* or pineapple. These practices were soon taken up by Europeans. When preparing a prospectus meant to attract investors and settlers for a new colony in Guiana, Walter Raleigh promised that

Those that have hot livers and love drink [shall find in Guiana] wine of *Pina*s, fitter for Princes than for drunkards . . . those that love Tobacco may here smoke themselves till they become bacon . . . and those that are

sweet lipped may fill themselves with *Pinas,* Princes of
all fruits.[3]

Raleigh was obliged to rewrite this passage before publication, in order to present a relatively sober image that would
appeal to financial backers and serious colonists, rather than
to adventurers and soldiers of fortune.

The line between fermented (alcoholic) and unferment-
ed juice was a fine one for two reasons. Firstly, fresh juice
fermented very quickly in the heat, a process that can almost
be seen happening in this description by Richard Ligon:

> The last and best sort of drink that this island [Barbados]
> or the world affords is the incomparable wine of pines.
> And is certainly the Nectar which the Gods drunk, and
> that is made of the pure juice of the fruit itself without
> commixture of water; or any other creature, having in
> itself a natural compound of all tastes excellent that the
> world can yield. This drink is too pure to keep long; in
> three or four days it will be fine, 'tis made by pressing the
> fruit and straining the liquor and it is kept in bottles.[4]

Modern equivalents of the simpler drinks of old are *pina*, in
which the pineapple peel and core are boiled with spices and
dark sugar and allowed to ferment, and sugar-cane *cachaça*
flavoured with pineapple.

The second reason why it was difficult to distinguish
between the two was because the juice was recognized to
have powers of its own, with an efficacy normally associated
with alcoholic drinks. Fresh, undiluted pineapple juice was
strong medicine, literally. The natives used it as a contracep-
tive, as a treatment for amoebic parasites and intestinal worms,
and to correct stomach disorders.[5] Today it is known that the

active agent in fresh pineapple juice and stalks is the proteolytic (able to break down molecules of protein) enzyme bromelain, which has many contemporary pharmaceutical, clinical and industrial applications. Its use in the Beverly Hills pineapple diet has been referred to, and its most common use in the home kitchen is as a meat tenderizer, either as a marinade or as an ingredient in cooking.

While most Europeans in the New World appreciated the way fresh pineapple juice could settle their stomachs and revive their flagging appetites, it was the alcoholic juice or wine that interested them. Oviedo, the man who loved pineapples, praised the sweetness of pineapple wine, at a time when a sweet taste was very highly prized. However, pineapple wine was so evanescent – quickly passing from fermented to spoiled – that interest shifted to pineapple rum, the wild child of the marriage of sugar and pineapple.

When Columbus brought sugar cane to the New World, he also brought the knowledge that the juice could be used to produce an alcoholic spirit.[6] When this knowledge, combined with indigenous techniques of fruit-based distillation and sugar refining, advanced sufficiently to produce large

Rum and pineapple cocktail. The simplest version is a mixture of pineapple rum and bitters, with the rum-soaked pineapple eaten at the end.

amounts of surplus sugar syrup, pineapple rum was born. The custom of putting slices of pineapple in the puncheons or rum casks was the origin of the term 'pineapple rum'.[7] Now largely forgotten in Europe and America, in its time pineapple rum was a highly desirable drink. Rum itself was a new spirit, previously unknown as a commercial product, and the addition of pineapple – then in its European heyday – added considerably to rum's attraction.

Out in the West Indies, rum making was rough and ready in the early days. Distilling was done in large vats or cisterns located in sheds and hovels that were open on all sides to the trade winds by the day and the land breezes by night. The ventilation was thought to promote natural fermentation, and if this slowed, a little clean, hot sand might be thrown in to stimulate effervescence. Above all, the character of West Indies rum came from 'the newness and freshness of the molasses drawn from the new-made sugar'.[8] Low-quality rum could be

Elite social drinking in England. The Prince of Wales presides at a carouse, punchbowl and pineapple on the table, in this English satirical print of 1786.

bitter and harsh, and pineapple could be used to soften it, while the fruit's savour blended beautifully with the rich mellowness of high-quality rum. Fruit- and spice-flavoured rums took over the place fruit-based wines had held in the West Indies since before the coming of sugar cane, but for export purposes fruit rum did not always travel well. The finest grades of aged pineapple rum from the West Indies were shipped to Britain and other parts of Europe, and America, from the eighteenth century onwards, but when fresh pineapple became available there, other methods of making pineapple rum and wine were found.

Brewing and distilling were home industries before the age of mass-production, and the making of wines, liqueurs, cordials, beers and shrubs were treasured domestic arts. Underripe imported pineapples could be peeled, sliced and layered with sugar in a stone jar, then topped up with rum, sealed and kept in a cool place to mature. The same technique is used today to make *rumtopf* or rum pot, in which fresh fruit and sugar are preserved in rum, except in this case it was the flavoured rum rather than the fruit that was of primary interest. A pineapple syrup to mix into rum or other spirits could be made by squeezing a half pint of fresh pineapple juice, and leaving it to ferment for two days with the residue of the fruit before straining. One pound of sugar was then added, and the mixture was boiled for three minutes, skimmed, strained clear and used for drinks like Gin Punch à la Burroughs (see recipe, p. 141). In 1870, the author of *Cooling Cups and Dainty Drinks* praised the rich and exquisite flavour of pineapples, 'a native of the West Indies and the tropics imported from thence to this country in great quantities' and gave a recipe for essence of pineapple, a mixture of ½ oz pineapple oil (butyric ether) and 3½ oz rectified spirit. At a time when juices were not easily available, these essences were used to flavour 'cups' like the Cider Nectar Cup à la Harold Littledale (see recipe, p. 140).

In Britain choice old pineapple rum from the West Indies continued to be sold by provisioners to the nobility and gentry, and used in drinks like Oxford Punch (see recipe, p. 141), but the appeal of pineapple wine went further down the social scale. The Reverend Mr Stiggins in Charles Dickens's *The Pickwick Papers* was 'easily prevailed upon to take another glass of hot pineapple rum and water, and a second, and a third'. Publicans and brewers found they could disguise the raw taste of cheap rum with pineapple, which they added as raw fruit, as a syrup or as a flavouring, making it ever-more widely available. The evidence is that this rough pineapple wine was highly popular. Victorian police notices are full of outbreaks of rowdy behaviour driven by an excess of pineapple rum, including one widely reported incident involving a bevy of women charged with drunkenness in London's Piccadilly. Before the judge, a Mrs Walker pleaded guilty to having been 'just elevated with one glass of the very best pineapple rum diluted with water – nothing more, upon my honour, sir', claiming in mitigation that it was 'Christmas time'.[9]

This behaviour would not have been tolerated in Honolulu. Hawaii was the great exception to the rule that sugar and rum are always found together. Due to missionary influence, a rum industry was never allowed to develop in Hawaii, Hawaiian canners' recipe books did not contain alcoholic recipes, and any home brewing had to be surreptitious. Much of it took place out in the sugar and pineapple fields, where 'pineapple swipe' was made. Reminiscent of the fruit spirits Columbus had encountered, making swipe involved selecting fine, ripe pineapples, cutting off the tops, chopping the fruit and adding sugar if necessary, replacing the crowns and letting the fruit

The development
of canned pineapple
juice in Hawaii in
1932 transformed
the market for
pineapples.

ferment in the sun for a few days. The result would, as locals said, 'swipe your head off'.

Prohibition – the ban of the manufacture, transportation and sale of alcohol – was in force in North America between 1919 and 1933. This suited the temperance faction on the Hawaiian islands, and it also presented the pineapple industry with a commercial opportunity, for in the absence of alcohol there was a new demand for non-alcoholic drinks. First soft drinks (sodas) were taken up, then canned fruit juice. The 'reducing diet craze of the early depression years' has also been seen as a factor in the rise of North American fruit juice sales generally.[10] In 1932, Dole's Hawaiian Pineapple Company developed a way of canning pineapple juice for the first time, doubling the potential market for the fruit.

Canned pineapple juice was convenient, easily transportable, benefitted from chilling in the new domestic refrigerators and lent itself well to both cooking and drinking. The canners introduced consumers to Hawaiian pineapple juice with lip-smacking descriptions:

> A sun-ripened pineapple eaten in Hawaii is a never-to-be-forgotten experience. Pick your own pineapple, hold it by the crown, and with one blow of the knife cut off the end; then slice the skin away and cut a big chunky slice. You will be amazed to see how the juice starts dripping from the pineapple the moment the knife touches it. And when you bite into the slice, the juice runs off your chin and onto the ground just as when you bite into a slice of watermelon; you will swallow as fast as you can to keep from choking on all the juice that runs down your throat. The flavour is the most delectable you ever tasted. Now you can buy this delicious juice in cans anywhere in the United States.[11]

The Pina Colada cocktail: rum, coconut cream and pineapple juice.

Dole then hired the prestigious advertising agency N. W. Ayer and Company to promote the Dole brand of Hawaiian pineapple juice in a national full-colour advertising campaign that linked the new juice with the luxury tourism of the times, and with exotic Hollywood films. This was swiftly followed by the publication of a collection of 'interesting recipes for

The Blue Hawaii cocktail: rum, pineapple juice and blue curaçao.

dishes to which Dole Pineapple Juice brings a new taste, a new freshness, a new delight'. Sales of pineapple juice rocketed. Published in 1935, *Morning, Noon and Night* contained recipes that used pineapple juice for fish and meats, fruit salads and cups, frozen desserts, and sauces and dressings. It also contained eighteen recipes for punches, fizzes and other drinks – none of them alcoholic.

This lack was soon remedied. Beyond the reach of Prohibition, this was the age of cocktails, which began as individual versions of the traditional island punches. Pineapple juice was a perfect ingredient for these heady mixtures. On the pineapple-growing islands of the West Indies, fresh pineapple juice had long been an ingredient in drinks. The Telegrafo, Havana's first hotel, was renowned for its fresh pineapple daiquiri, and 'Trader Vic' Bergeron waxed lyrical about the Pino Frio cocktail created at La Florida bar, also in Havana, which involved the use of an ingenious machine. As he described it:

> Practically every corner dispensary in Havana, whether ice cream parlor, cigarette counter, or a common saloon, has a big gadget on the counter that's a cross between a sewing machine and a coffee grinder. Somewhere or other those Cubans stick a pineapple in the contraption, turn a crank to beat hell, and out comes the best pineapple juice this side of Hawaii. They dump a couple of shots of rum and some shaved ice along with the pineapple juice in a hand shaker, twirl it fancy-like a few times, and dump it into a glass. Result: the most refreshing drink you've ever tasted.[12]

Canned Hawaiian pineapple juice made this machine obsolete, and also pushed pineapple rum into the background because the juice could now easily be added to plain rums. As soon as

Prohibition was over, a craze for rum and pineapple cocktails broke out, which continues to the present day, with the more opulent versions served in hollowed out fresh pineapples or ceramic pineapple goblets. Trader Vic invented the iconic Mai Tai,[13] which originally contained neither pineapple juice nor fresh pineapple spear, but which is now always served with both. His rival Don the Beachcomber invented the Missionary's Downfall, a combination of rum, lime juice, peach liqueur and pineapple. The famous Pina Colada – a mixture of rum, coconut cream and pineapple juice – was created in Puerto Rico by Ramon Marrero, the bartender at the Caribe Hilton in San Juan. However, like all the best concoctions, most pineapple drinks – with or without alcohol – seem simply to have invented themselves.

6

Global Pineapple

Even in their heyday, the Hawaiian pineapple growers had competitors, prime among them producers in the British Empire. By the end of the nineteenth century Britain had become reliant on food imports, and it was economically important that as many of these imports as possible should come from within the Empire, rather than from foreign sources. Recognized as the best, canned Hawaiian pineapple was offered for sale in elite British emporiums like Fortnum & Mason, but policy dictated that other, British sources be sought to supply the general market.

Apart from the West Indies, pineapples were already under cultivation in many British colonies as a result of dissemination – both accidental and planned – during the ages of discovery and empire-formation. The fruit flourished in northern Australia, South Africa and British Malaya, and in the late nineteenth and early twentieth centuries intensive pineapple growing was encouraged in all three of these countries. In Malaya, for example, pineapples were planted between the fledgling rubber trees, as well as in fields of their own, while visitors to Australia remarked on the contrast between the English-looking fruit orchards of Victoria and New South Wales, and the fields of Northern Queensland, with their 'emerald green tracts of sugar cane and ruddy acres of rose-tinted pineapple'.[1]

In order to promote British Empire goods and increase Empire productivity, the Empire Marketing Board (EMB) was established in 1926.[2] The EMB commissioned striking posters of Empire goods from leading artists of the day, provided shops with display material for Empire products and carried out national advertising campaigns. It also devised recipes that included a special Christmas pudding using only Empire fruits, which was presented to the king, George V; the recipe was shared with the public and quickly become the most famous recipe in the world. The EMB held high-profile formal dinners with menus comprising only foods produced within the Empire, such as this 1928 seasonal menu for the month of August:

> Melon Prince of Wales
> Irish clear soup or Montreal Cream Soup
> Brill with Pontac Wine Sauce
> Saddle of Sussex Lamb Empire
> Sorbet Zanzibar
> Worthing Asparagus with Australian Butter
> Surrey Chicken Britannia with Sudan Salad
> Natal Pineapple Veiled with Queensland Sugar
> Dominion Fruits
> Tanganyika Coffee[3]

The EMB published the recipes for distribution to the public, and the sale of Empire products rose. Out in the colonies, the expansion of pineapple growing and canning led to increased consumption and new recipes. The pavlova, a combination of meringue, whipped cream and fruit, whose invention is disputed by Australia and New Zealand, was

A Chinese takeaway standard: sweet-and-sour pork with pineapple and green peppers.

created in honour of the ballerina Anna Pavlova, who visited the Antipodes in 1926 and was presented with a pavlova made with pineapple (see recipe, p. 138).

While fresh pineapples had long been used in Southeast Asian cookery, the new availability of the canned fruit resulted in it coming into wider use in terms of season and distribution, as it had in North America and Europe, where it also appeared increasingly in Chinese restaurants in 'oriental' dishes specially created for the Western palate, notably the many versions of sweet-and-sour pineapple chicken and pineapple pork.

The Second World War destroyed the pineapple operations in Malaya, Taiwan and the Philippines, but they were rebuilt when peace returned. Australia and South Africa expanded their pineapple production in the post-Second World War period, and efforts were made to grow the pineapple in East and West Africa. In the 1960s, pressed by rising costs, competition and an increasingly globalized market, Hawaiian producers began to move their operations into Southeast

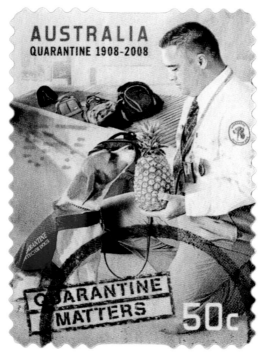

Protecting the pineapple; quarantine checks safeguard against the import of pests that would damage the Australian pineapple industry, commemorated on this postage stamp.

Asia and the Philippines. Here they were able to take advantage of a history that stretched back to the early days of European exploration, which they built on by introducing a new breed of pineapple – the MD2 Gold, developed by the Pineapple Research Institute in Hawaii and now the premier commercial strain.

Before the arrival of the Europeans, the natives of the New World employed pineapple fibres for weaving, netting and rope-making. Similar applications developed wherever the pineapple travelled, notably in the Philippines, where the fine, light *pina* cloth – woven from fibres scraped from pineapple leaves – is used to make the traditional formal *barong*

Pineapple massage oil.

tagalog or embroidered overshirt. There are many new clinical, complementary, cosmetic, pharmaceutical and other uses of the pineapple, including as a biofuel, but its main use is still in food and drink, and numerous new applications have developed in the mass-produced ready-meal market. Here the pineapple's presence is often invisible, since it is mixed with other ingredients in concentrated form to enhance the flavour, sweetness and sourness of ready meals, beverages and desserts in particular.

Today pineapple is a global product, one of the great commodities of modern transnational corporations led by Dole Food Company Inc., now the largest producer of fresh fruit and vegetables in the world. After bananas, the pineapple is the most widely eaten tropical fruit, sold fresh, frozen, juiced, canned, concentrated, puréed and dehydrated, and as essences, powder, flavourings and syrups. The top pineapple producers are, in descending but ever-changing order: Brazil, where the pineapple came from; the Philippines, Thailand, Costa Rica and Indonesia. China, Kenya, Nigeria, India, Ivory Coast and Mexico are increasing their production, and commercial pineapple growing continues in Central and South America and the Caribbean. The Asian countries generally specialize in canned and processed pineapple exports, with the other countries tending to focus on fresh fruit exports. Some countries, like Brazil, consume much of their produce internally, and old Empire producers like Australia and South Africa also have large domestic markets.

Japanese pineapple *kanten* dessert.

It is impossible to go around the world today without encountering the pineapple in some distinctive culinary or drinkable form. Unusual recipes can be tracked down, consumed, picture-shared and commented on via social media and the Internet. Here are some highlights to look out for when undertaking digital and real-world quests of your own. They give a mere taste of what is out there, for which the earlier chapters have provided history and context.

In New Zealand you can find the iconic Kiwi sweet – Pineapple Lumps – a chewy pineapple treat regarded as a national treasure. Also look out for pineapple pavlova, and New Zealand lamb marinated in pineapple juice before grilling. In Australia, pineapple fruitcakes – like the old Empire fruitcakes but using only Australian tropical fruits – and pineapple bread are Christmas and teatime delights. The Philippines have a large repertoire of pineapple recipes, including the popular *Pininyahang Manok*, chicken and pineapple stew, and in the South Pacific try Tahitian *poisson cru ananas* – fresh tuna marinated in coconut milk, lime juice and pineapple.

In Japan, beautifully cut and presented pieces of perfectly ripe fruit are the preferred mode, but a speciality worth seeking out is pineapple-flavoured *kanten,* a Japanese kind of firm gelatin.

In Southeast Asia, be sure to seek out Nonya or Peranakan cuisine. The Nonya are descendants of early Chinese immigrants to Penang, Malacca, Singapore and Indonesia who developed a Chinese/Malay cuisine in which pineapple figures often, a favourite dish being *Udang Masak Lemak Nenas*, prawn and pineapple curry.

Throughout Southeast Asia and in China, it was customary to eat pineapple tart at New Year because the Chinese characters for the tart are similar to those for 'prosperity', so it was a lucky food to eat at the start of a new cycle. Pineapple

Chinese pineapple tarts for New Year.

cakes are eaten in Taiwan at New Year for the same reason, and pineapple-shaped lanterns in the auspicious red colour are used as decorations during the festival.

The pineapple was taken to Southeast Asia from the New World at the same time as the manioc. The Asian manner of dealing with the manioc root was to process it very fine as tapioca, which is mixed with pineapple and sometimes coconut to produce cool, soothing puddings and pineapple-flavoured *boba* or bubble tea. In Cambodia, the dish to search out is 'sour soup' with pineapple, pork and coconut milk. One of the great culinary mysteries is why India – which received pineapples early, and where they grew well – did not take up the fruit, but pineapple fritters as eaten in the heyday of the British Raj are worth seeking out or recreating, and India produces a fine selection of pineapple chutneys and sambals.

In China, pineapple was preserved in sugar syrup as a luxury when it first came to the country, and it is still made in that way like ginger in syrup, but since China became a pineapple-producing nation fresh pineapple has become a popular street food. Pineapples are carved into fancy shapes, placed on sticks and sold from carts as snacks by street vendors. Whole pineapples for home consumption are also sold widely.

In South Africa, where pineapples were introduced by the Dutch, there is 'Cape Malay' cookery, which reflects colonial influences from Southeast Asia and India, including dishes such as *bobotie* with pineapple (curried meat and fruit with a creamy topping), and also contemporary fusion cookery in which South African-grown pineapple is used liberally as an ingredient and a condiment, for example in pineapple and kudu kebabs, in which kudu (antelope) meat is marinated in fresh pineapple juice to tenderize it, then grilled on a spit with pineapple chunks. In 1639 a voyager to the coast of Guinea in West Africa reported that the natives there relished the pineapple (introduced by the Portuguese), which they ate fresh and also cooked in palm oil, a practice continued today where the

Lucky pineapple Chinese New Year decorations.

Hawaii pineapple in flames.

Pineapple farm in South Africa, featuring a large artificial pineapple as a tourist attraction.

cooked fruit is eaten alone or mixed with spices, meat and plantains. A particularly delicious dish is the famous West African peanut 'soup' or stew – a spicy tomato, chilli and peanut gravy with chicken or meat – to which pineapple can be added.

In Europe the Dutch, who were the first to grow the pineapple in the Old World, continue to make superb pineapple *konfyt* or jam, and also enjoy pineapple as part of their colonial culinary heritage. The pineapple is an ingredient in Dutch curries, and in their famous *rijsttafel* or 'rice table', an array of Indonesian dishes.

Germany has its pineapple cakes and tarts – *ananas-kuchen* and *ananas-törtchen* – as well as sauerkraut with pineapple and summer *bowle,* a fruit punch with pineapple, while in France tropical fruits have long been incorporated into classic desserts like *crème brûlée ananas.* Look out for pineapple vinegar in Spain. Vinegar was one of the staples the first settlers took to the New

World. There, it was combined with pineapple to make an unusual and refreshing condiment that quickly became as popular in Spain as it was in Mexico.

With this very quick cook's tour we are back in the New World where the journey of the pineapple began. The Caribbean offers a world of breakfast-to-dinner pineapple treats and drinks, including pineapple jam, pineapple cakes and pies, pineapple cooked with brown sugar and sweet potatoes, pot-roast pork with pineapple and allspice, and heady pineapple punches. Along the Pacific coast of Central America, where there is fine seafood and pineapples flourish, the two come together in tangy seafood salads. In Argentina, pineapple salsa is an indispensible accompaniment to *churrasco* or barbecued meat, while in Brazil, homeland of the pineapple, wonderful ripe fruit is sold in all the markets, and the rich, sweet cakes and desserts of the colonial period continue to be made, among them the creamy pineapple pudding known as *doce de abacaxi*.

The recipes that follow present history on a plate and in a glass, and the foregoing account has shown when, why and how the fruit of kings became the queen of fruits. To end, I can only agree with Oviedo, the man who loved pineapple as much as I do. 'My pen and my words', he wrote, 'cannot depict such exceptional qualities, nor appropriately celebrate this fruit'.[4] Let the pineapple speak for itself. Go and treat yourself to one now.

Recipes

Eating the Pineapple

Frederick Nutt's Pineapple Confectionery
— from Frederick Nutt, *The Complete Confectionery* (London, 1819)

Frederick Nutt was a British society confectioner who worked for
the celebrated Negri and Witten at the Sign of the Pineapple in
London's Berkeley Square. The full sequence of his pineapple
recipes is given here, showing how elite confectioners of the
Georgian and Victorian periods used the fruit. The ice cream is
excellent; not over-rich, it can be made in an ice-cube tray and
benefits from the addition of chopped candied pineapple to taste.

Preserved Pineapple Chips, Wet Take the top of the stalk of the
pineapple, chip off the ends of the outsides and the bottoms of
them; cut the pineapples in slices about the thickness of the fifth
part of an inch; take an earthen deep pan and one pound of sugar;
lay some sugar at the bottom of the pan, then a layer of the pieces
of pine, but not over the other; then put another layer of sugar,
then another of pine, and so on till your pan is almost full; at
the top put a good deal of sugar pretty deep; cover them up with
paper and let them stand till you see the sugar is almost melted;
let them and the syrup boil half an hour, then put them in the
same pan again, the next day give them another boil, and so

continue eight days, then drain all the syrup from them entirely; if the syrup is too clodden, just dip the chips in a little water; then wipe them and lay them on your sieve to dry; mind the sieve is quite dry; as you put them into the stove, dust a little very fine powdered sugar through a cloth bag over them, put them in the stove and let them remain there till you think they will not give or be stickey; then put them in your drawers or box with clean white paper around them.

Pineapple Syrup Drain the syrup from your pineapple chips, when you are going to dry them that are preserved, as you will see in your receipt of pineapple chips; boil the syrup three or four times, and put it into your bottles while warm. Cork and bladder them the next day.

Pineapple Ice Cream Take one gill and a half of pineapple syrup, put into a basin and squeeze in one lemon and a half, add one pint of cream, make it palatable, then put it in your freezing pot and freeze till as thick as butter. If you would have it in the shape of a pine, take the shape and fill it then lay half a sheet of brown paper over the mold before you put it into the ice and let it remain some time, and be careful no water gets into the shape.

Ananas à la Créole
— from André Simon, ed., *A Concise Encyclopedia of Gastronomy* (London, 1942)

From the French West Indian colonies, this is the original recipe for a dish that became very popular in the early days of canned fruit cocktail with pineapple, mixed with dessicated or dried coconut, under the name of 'Ambrosia'. This version, with everything fresh, really is ambrosial.

Take a medium size pineapple and, with a silver knife and fork, scoop out the inside of the fruit and mash into a pulp. Skin three bananas and three oranges, slice the bananas into rings and mash the oranges, having removed pips and inner skin. Mix with the pineapple. Take a small fresh coconut and grate it finely and mix with the other fruit, together with sugar to taste and the juice of a lemon. Keep in the refrigerator for some time before serving.

Pineapple Tart
— from Richard Bradley, *Country Housewife and Lady's Director* (London, 1732)

This early dish (1732) was eaten in Britain and the American colonies during the colonial period; note the reference to flavouring wine with pineapples.

To make a tart of the Ananas or Pine-apple from Barbadoes. Take a Pine-apple and twist off its Crown: then pare it free from the Knots, and cut it in Slices about half an inch thick; then stew it with a little Canary Wine or Madeira Wine and some Sugar, till it is thoroughly hot, and it will distribute its Flavour to the wine much better than anything we can add to it. When it is as one would have it, take it from the Fire, and when it is cool, put it into a sweet Paste, with its Liquor, and bake it gently, a little while, and when it comes from the Oven, pour Cream over it (if you have it) and serve it either hot or cold.

Pineapple Pudding
— Marie Kimball, *Thomas Jefferson's Cook Book* (Charlottesville, VA, 1938)

This is another pineapple recipe from the American colonial period, from the family cookbook of the third President of the United States, Thomas Jefferson.

Peel the pineapple, taking care to get all the specs out, and grate it. Take its weight in sugar and half its weight in butter. Rub the butter and sugar to a cream and stir them into the pineapple. Add five well beaten eggs and 1 cup of cream. It may be baked with or without the pastry crust.

Pineapple-Lime-Cottage Cheese Gelatin Salad

The invention of canning led to a fad for jellied pineapple salads. There are many versions of this kitsch dish.

1 (3 oz) package lime gelatin
¾ cup boiling water
1 small can crushed pineapple, undrained
1 cup cottage cheese
½ cup whipping cream
¼ cup finely chopped celery

Dissolve gelatin in boiling water, add ½ cup reserved pineapple syrup or juice from can. Chill until thickened but not set firm. Fold in pineapple, cottage cheese, celery and whipped cream. Chill until set firm.

Pineapple Minute Tapioca
— from Minute Tapioca Company Inc., *A Cook's Tour with Minute Tapioca* (Orange, MA, 1931)

This is a retro recipe from the 1930s, teaming pineapple with a great dessert favourite of the period, tapioca.

½ cup Minute Tapioca
¼ teaspoon salt
4 cups hot pineapple juice and water
½ cup sugar
1 cup canned pineapple, grated or finely cut

Add Minute Tapioca and salt to pineapple juice and water, and cook in it double boiler 15 minutes or until tapioca is clear, stirring frequently. Add sugar and pineapple and chill. Serve with whipped cream, serves 8. If fresh fruit is used, it should be sweetened to taste and allowed to stand ½ hour or more. Any fruit juice may be used as part of liquid.

Boston Baked Beans with Pineapple
— from Association of Hawaiian Pineapple Canners, *Hawaiian Pineapple as 100 Good Cooks Serve It* (San Francisco, CA, 1926)

In culinary terms it is hard not to think of this dish as a lovely island girl seducing a missionary.

Soak 1 quart small pea beans overnight. Parboil the beans in fresh boiling water for 10 minutes. Drain and add 1 cup water. Mix 1 teaspoon salt, 1 teaspoon dry mustard, ½ teaspoon soda and 1 tablespoon molasses in another cup water. Place one onion stuck with 5 cloves in the bottom of bean pot. Add a layer of beans, then 1½ slices of Hawaiian Pineapple cut in quarters. Repeat with beans and like amount pineapple with a top layer of beans. Score ¼ pound salt pork in ½ inch cuts through the rind, wash thoroughly, and bury to the rind in beans. Pour seasonings in water over all. Bake in slow oven (250–300F) for 5 or 6 hours. Keep cover on until the last hour and renew water as needed. Serve with button radishes and sharply sour pickle.

Pineapple Upside-down Cake
— from Del Monte Corporation, *Luau Favourites and Island Recipes* (1975)

If you do not use cake mixes, substitute your favourite yellow cake recipe for the yellow cake mix suggested in this recipe.

1 can (20 oz) Del Monte Sliced Pineapple
½ cup margarine or butter
1 cup firmly packed brown sugar

⅓ cup coconut
⅓ cup macadamia nuts
5 maraschino cherries, halved
1 pkg (18½ oz) yellow cake mix

1) Melt margarine or butter in 13 × 9 inch pan. Add sugar.
2) Arrange fruit, coconut, nut and cherries in sugar mixture in a decorative pattern, cherry halves inside pineapple rings.
3) Prepare cake mix as package directs. Spread over fruit.
4) Bake at 35°F, 45 to 50 minutes or until tests done.
5) Cool 5 minutes; invert onto large serving dish.
6) Serve warm or cold. 12 servings.

Pineapple Coconut Pudding

This classic Brazilian colonial dessert uses the condensed milk that is a popular staple in the tropics. It is modelled on European trifles, but with an exotic twist.

1 (410 g) condensed milk
1½ cups (340 ml) milk
2 egg yolks, beaten
3 tablespoons cornflour
1 teaspoon pure vanilla essence
1 plain sponge cake layer, pound cake or Madeira cake
1 cup (225 ml) pineapple juice
⅓ cup (150 ml) dark rum
1 (425 g) can sliced pineapple, drained
¾ cup (60 g) dessicated coconut
1 cup (225 ml) whipping cream, whipped
Maraschino cherries to decorate

In a double boiler, mix the condensed milk, milk, egg yorks, cornflour and vanilla. Cook over hot water, stirring constantly until thick. Continue to cook with stirring for 10 minutes, then remove from the heat and allow to cool.

Cut the sponge layer or pound or Madeira cake into pieces and place in the bottom of a bowl suitable for trifles. Mix the pineapple juice and rum, sprinkle over the cake and cover with half the cooled custard mixture and half the drained pineapple pieces, cut up. Sprinkle with half the coconut. Then cover with remaining half of the custard, finish with a layer of whipped cream and decorate the top with the remaining pineapple, coconut and cherries.

Like trifles, this pudding benefits from being allowed to sit in the fridge for a few hours, for the flavours to blend and the rum and pineapple juice to moisten the cake.

Island Pineapple Spareribs

This is an old-style (*kamaaina*) dish from the Territorial period of Hawaiian culinary history.

3 lb (1.4 kg) spare ribs cut into 2 in (5 cm) lengths
¾ cup (150 g) sugar
½ cup (110 ml) white vinegar
¼ cup (55 ml) sake
1 tablespoon soy sauce
1 cup (225 ml) pineapple juice
1 tablespoon fresh ginger, in slices
1 tablespoon salt
4 tablespoons cornstarch (cornflour)
1 small can (225 ml) pineapple chunks or slices,
or fresh pineapple
cooking oil

Dredge the spare ribs in 3 tablespoons of the cornstarch. Brown in batches in oil. Mix together the sugar, vinegar, sake, soy sauce, pineapple juice and remaining cornstarch. Put the browned spare ribs in a roasting pan, and pour the mixture sauce over them. Bake in an oven preheated to 180°C/350°F for 1½ hours, basting frequently.

Pineapple Pavlova

For the pavlova:
3 egg whites
1 teaspoon vanilla essence
2 teaspoons cornflour
6 oz (175 g) caster sugar
2 teaspoons white wine vinegar

For the filling
3 egg yolks
½ tablespoon butter
½ teaspoon grated lemon rind
1 tablespoon sugar
1 teaspoon lemon juice
1 13 oz (370 g) can crushed pineapple

½ pint (300 ml) whipping cream, to finish

For the pavlova, beat the egg whites until stiff, then add the sugar gradually continuing to beat until smooth. Fold in the vanilla, cornflour and vinegar. Spread the mixture into an 8 in (20 cm) round shell on a greased and lined baking sheet. Make the sides of the shell higher than the middle. Bake for 1 hour in an oven preheated to 150°C/300°F. Put all ingredients for the filling into a double boiler or thick pan and gently cook until thickened, stirring continuously. Cool, and pour into the centre of the meringue round. To finish, whip the whipping cream and spread it over the top of the filled meringue shell. Decorate with additional pineapple pieces.

Sweet Sour Pineapple Chicken

More 'Chinatown' than authentic Chinese, this is typical of the 'sweet-sour' dishes popular in Chinese American restaurants through the 1960's. Tinned water chestnuts, drained and sliced, were sometimes added, as were thinly sliced carrots, cut in rounds and lightly sautéed. For a retro touch, a green bell pepper – seeded, cut into chunks and lightly sautéed – can be included, but the taste of the pepper tends to drown the other flavours.

2 skinless, boneless chicken breasts, sliced into 6–8 pieces each
2 tsp cornflour (cornstarch)
1 tsp sherry
1 tsp water
1 clove garlic, minced
1 tsp fresh ginger, pounded and then minced
2 tsp cornflour (cornstarch)
1 tbsp soy sauce
1 tbsp sherry
1 tbsp hoisin sauce
1 tsp lemon juice
¾ cup canned pineapple chunks
¼ cup pineapple juice
3 tbsp vegetable oil

Combine 2 tsp cornstarch, 1 tsp sherry and 1 tsp water, coat the chicken slices with the mixture, place in bowl, cover and chill for half an hour. Heat oil in a wok or heavy pan, add chicken and stir-fry for two minutes. Add pineapple, cover and cook for 3 minutes until the chicken is done through. Remove chicken and pineapple and keep warm. Combine garlic, ginger, 2 tsp cornstarch, soy sauce, 1 tbsp sherry, hoisin sauce, pineapple juice and lemon juice. Add to wok or pan, stir until sauce thickens and is hot. Pour over warm chicken and pineapple chunks and serve with plain white rice.

Pineapple *Konfyt*
—from *Cape Cookery* by A. G. Hewitt (1890)

The Dutch of the Cape were renowned for their fresh fruit preserves or *konfyts*. Like many old recipes, this one uses the outer peel of the pineapple, to give additional flavour. The pineapple should be well washed before peeling and using.

Peel the pineapples, cut them in slices ½ an inch in thickness. Put the parings into a lined saucepan with water, and boil them up. Stain off the water, and put it with the sliced pineapple into a preserving pan, add sufficient water to float the pineapple and boil till soft. Take out the fruit with a slice so as not to break it, and let it drain. Make the syrup, using the water in which the pineapple has boiled. When it begins to thicken, put in the pineapple, and boil till it is quite transparent.

Drinking the Pineapple

Recipes for contemporary cocktails based on pineapples abound on the Internet, but for the historically minded the first three recipes come from a British book of 1870.

Cider Nectar Cup à la Harold Littledale
— from William Terrington, *Cooling Cups and Dainty Drinks* (London, 1870)

1 quart cider
1 bottle soda-water
1 glass of sherry
1 small glass of brandy
juice of ½ lemon (strained)
¼ of a lemon rubbed on sugar cube
sugar and nutmeg to taste
a sprig of verbena

Flavour it to taste with extract of pine-apple; strain and ice well. This cup well deserves all the praise it has received.

Oxford Punch

Put the thinly-pared peelings of 4 lemons and 2 Seville oranges into a mortar containing ½ lb loaf-sugar, which beat up into a smooth mass; into which squeeze the juice of the fruit, adding juice of 4 sweet oranges and ½ pint of water; strain the mixture into a jug (standing close to the fire); add 1 pint of calves-foot jelly, which thoroughly incorporate; pour in 2 quarts of boiling water, ½ pint syrup, teaspoonful of orange-flower water, wine-glass of Curaçao, ½ pint of sherry, pint of Cognac brandy, pint of pine-apple rum, quart of orange-shrub; stir well together. Serve hot.

Gin Punch à la Burroughs

Juice of 1 lemon
1 gill of pineapple syrup
1 pint of gin
1 quart of tea (green)

If preferred as a cool punch, use broken ice instead of tea.

Pineapple Julep
—from *Cassell's Dictionary of Cookery* (*c.* 1890)

Pare a very ripe pineapple with as little waste as possible, and cut it into thin slices. Lay these in a large bowl and strain over them the juice of two sweet oranges. Pour in a quarter of a pint of maraschino liqueur, a quarter of a pint of gin and a quarter of a pint of raspberry syrup and mix thoroughly. Just before serving, add a bottle of sparkling Moselle and a tumblerful of shaved ice.

Iced Pineapple Coffee

— from Hawaiian Pineapple Company Ltd, *Morning, Noon and Night*
(Honolulu, 1935)

⅜ cup sugar
¾ cup water
¾ teaspoon grated orange rind
3 cups cold coffee
¾ cup Dole Hawaiian Pineapple Juice
¾ cup cream
crushed ice

Boil the sugar, water and orange rind together for 10 minutes. Cool, strain and add cold coffee. Just before serving, add pineapple juice and cream. Serve in tall glasses filled with crushed ice. 6 servings.

Hawaiian Pineapple Mint Iced Tea

Make tea to your taste and dip mint leaves in it for three minutes. For each 14 oz glass add the juice of half a lemon, 1 tablespoon pineapple juice and 3 teaspoons sugar. Place in a blender or shaker and mix well. Chill before serving over ice, garnished with a mint sprig and pineapple spear.

References

Introduction: Origins and Discovery

1 Ferdinand Columbo, *The Life of The Admiral Christopher Columbus by his Son Ferdinand*, trans. and annotated by Benjamin Keen (New Brunswick, NJ, 1959), pp. 111–12.
2 Ibid., p. 72.
3 Kenneth G. Rohrbach, Freddy Leaf and Geo Coppens d'Eckenbrugge, 'History, Distribution and World Production', in *The Pineapple: Botany, Production and Uses* (Honolulu, IL, 2003), ed. Duane Philip Bartholomew with Robert E. Paul and Kenneth E. Rohrbach, pp. 1–2.
4 Gonzalo Fernandez de Oviedo y Caldez, *Historia General y Natural de las Indias*, translation of a manuscript in the Huntington Library (HM 117), San Marino, California, in J. L. Collins, *The Pineapple: Botany, Cultivation and Utilization* (London, 1960), pp. 9–11.

1 Fruit of Kings

1 Peter Martyr D'Anghera, *De Orbe Novo: The Eight Decades of Peter Martyr d'Anghera, translated with Notes and Introduction by Francis Augustus MacNutt* (New York, 1912), vol. 1, pp. 262–3.
2 In J. L. Collings, *The Pineapple: Botany, Cultivation and Utilization* (London, 1960), p. 12.

3 Pierre Pomet, *A Compleat History of Drugs* [1712], cited in Fran Beauman, *The Pineapple* (London, 2005), p. 38.

4 Joyce Lorimer, ed., *Sir Walter Ralegh's 'Discoverie of Guiana'* (London, 2006).

5 Thomas Verney, quoted in Aubrey Gwynn, 'Indentured Servants and Negro Slaves in Barbados', *Studies: An Irish Quarterly Review,* XIX/74 (1930), p. 290.

6 John Locke, *An Essay Concerning Human Understanding*, Book III, chap. 4.

7 Richard Ligon, *True and Exact History of the Island of Barbados* (1673), p. 84.

8 Elizabeth Hall, 'The Plant Collections of an Eighteenth-century Virtuoso', *Garden History*, XIV/1 (Spring 1986), pp. 6–31; see also Gregory King, *Natural and Political Observations and Conclusions upon the State and Condition of England* (London, 1696).

9 John Gabriel Stedman, *Narrative of a Five Years' Expedition to Surinam in 1790* (London, 1796), vol. II, p. 212.

10 Edward Ives, *Voyage from England to India in the year 1754* (London, 1773), p 57.

11 Christopher Thacker, *'La Manière de montrer les jardins à Versailles* by Louis XIV and Others', *Garden History*, I/1 (September 1972), p. 55.

12 Noël-Antoine Pluche, *Spectacle de la Nature*, English edition (London, 1737), vol. II, pp. 178–9.

13 See 'The Yew Tree Ball: Chateau of Versailles', at http://en.chateauversailles.fr, accessed May 2012.

14 *The Mirror*, vol. III (Edinburgh, 1783), p. 205.

15 Fran Beauman, 'The King of Fruits', *Cabinet*, 23 (Fall 2006).

16 David Hume, *A Treatise of Human Nature* (London, 1739).

17 Sophie Coe, *America's First Cuisines* (Austin, TX, 1994), p. 41.

18 Susan Campbell, 'The Genesis of Queen Victoria's Great New Kitchen Garden', *Garden History*, XII/2, p. 104.

19 Kathryn Jones, *For the Royal Table* (London, 2008), p. 72.

20 Jessica Rutherford, *A Prince's Passion: A History of the Brighton Pavilion* (Brighton, 2003).

2 Mapping the Pineapple

1 G. W. Johnson, *The Pineapple: Its Culture, Use and History* (London, 1847), p. 1.

2 André L. Simon, *A Concise Encyclopedia of Gastronomy* (London, 1947), p. 55.

3 Ferdinand Columbo, *The Life of The Admiral Christopher Columbus by his Son Ferdinand*, trans. and annotated by Benjamin Keen (New Brunswick, NJ, 1959), p. 253.

4 Kathleen Ann Myers and Nina M. Scott, *Fernandez de Oviedo's Chronicle of America* (Austin, TX, 2007), p. 161.

5 J. L. Collins, *The Pineapple: Botany, Cultivation and Utilization* (London, 1960); Berthold Laufer, *The American Plant Migration* (Chicago, IL, 1938).

6 Elizabeth A. Standen, 'The Story of the Emperor of China: A Beauvais Tapestry Series', at http://metmuseum.org, accessed May 2012.

7 Kaori O'Connor, 'Beyond "Exotic Groceries"; Tapioca-Cassava, a Hidden Commodity of Empire', Commodities of Empire working papers no. 10, www.open.ac.uk, accessed April 2013; also Kaori O'Connor, 'Beyond Exotic Groceries', in *Global Histories, Imperial Commodities*, ed. Jonathan Curry-Machado (London, 2013); Rebecca Earle, '"If You Eat Their Food": Diets and Bodies in Early Colonial Spanish America', *American Historical Review*, cxv/3 (June 2010), pp. 688–713.

8 Sophie Coe, *America's First Cuisines* (Austin, TX, 1994), p. 93.

9 R. B. Cunningham Graham, *Bernal Díaz del Castillo* (London, 1915), p. 20.

10 Richard Ligon, *True and Exact History of the Island of Barbados* (London, 1673), p. 83.

11 Rochefort quoted in Steven J. Taussig and Stanley Batkin, 'Bromelain, the Enzyme Complex of Pineapple and Its Clinical Application, an Update', *Journal of Ethnopharmacology*, 22 (1988), p. 192.

12 Sidney Mintz, *Sweetness and Power* (New York, 1985), p. 32.

13 Gilberto Freyre, *Açúcar* (Recife, 1987).

14 Coe, *America's First Cuisines*, p. 229.

15 Jeffrey M. Pilcher, *Que Vivan los Tamales!* (Albuquerque, NM, 1998).

16 Full recipe can be found in Elizabeth Lambert Ortiz, *The Complete Book of Mexican Cooking* (New York, 1992), p. 190.

17 Coe, *America's First Cuisines*, p. 229.

18 Charles Leslie, writing in 1740, in *The Times*, 24 May 1910, p. 34, col. F.

19 Donald Jackson, ed., *The Diaries of George Washington*, vol 1: *1748–65* (Charlottesville, VA, 1976), p. 87.

20 Sarah F. McMahon, 'A Comfortable Subsistence: The Changing Composition of Diet in Rural New England, 1620–1840', *The William and Mary Quarterly*, third series, vol. XLII, no. 1 (January 1985), pp. 26–65.

21 Michael Olmert, 'The Hospitable Pineapple', *Colonial Williamsburg* journal, vol. XX, no. 2 (Winter 1997–1998), p. 50.

22 The information about pineapples at the Governor's Palace in Colonial Williamsburg comes from William Marshman's manuscript, 'Governor's Palace Kitchen Account Book, 1769–1771'. Rockefeller Library owns microfilm and a transcript of the original; John A Caramia, 'Wages and Prices', *Colonial Williamsburg Interpreter*, XXVII/2 (Summer 1996), pp. 24–7; 20 shillings = £1 Sterling [from a 1772 manuscript entitled 'Arithmetic' compiled by John Graves of Culpeper, later Madison County, Virginia, quoted in Mrs Philip Wallace Hiden, 'The Money of Colonial Virginia', *Virginia Magazine of History and Biography*, LI/1 (January 1943), pp. 36–54. Courtesy Juleigh Muirhead Clark, Colonial Williamsburg Foundation].

23 'The Senator Weds', *Life* (28 September 1953), p. 45.

24 Wedding menu courtesy of the John F. Kennedy Presidential Library, personal communication with the author.

25 Philip Morin Freneau, 'The Beauties of Santa Cruz', in *The Poems of Philip Frenau* (Princeton, NJ, 1902), vol. 1, p. 299.

3 Queen Pine

1 Charles Lamb, 'A Dissertation Upon Roast Pig', in *Elia* (London, 1823), pp. 284–5.

2 'Adelaide Gallery', *The Times*, 13 June 1837, p. 6, col. B.

3 'A New Vegetable Fibre', *Morning Post*, London, 16 June 1837, p. 7.

4 G. W. Johnson, *The Pineapple: Its Culture, Use and History* (London, 1847), pp. 22–44.

5 C. Ludger, Preface, in Johan Philipp Siebenkees, *The Life of Bianca Capello, Wife of Francesco de Medici, Grand Duke of Tuscany* (Liverpool, 1797), pp. ii–iii.

6 'Christmas and the Fruit Markets', *The Times*, 22 December 1898, p. 9.

7 J. Robson, 'The Fruit and Kitchen Gardens', *Journal of Horticulture*, XXII (1872), p. 455.

8 *Pall Mall Gazette* in *The London Reader,* 1 October 1873, pp. 474–5.

9 'Confectioners Botany', *All the Year Round*, 10 August 1861, pp. 462–4.

10 Mrs A. B. Marshall, *Fancy Ices* (London, 1894), pp. 102–03.

11 Henry Mayhew, Letter XII, Tuesday November 27, 1849, Labour and the Poor 1849–1850, *Morning Chronicle*. Original prices modernized (4d=4 pence).

12 'London Street Markets: Paradox of Fruit Prices', *The Times*, 4 August 1928, p. 14.

13 Charles H. Fox, 'Bottled Fruit', *The Times*, 2 August 1910, p. 7.

14 'Lovers of Verbal Accuracy Have Frequently Complained', editorial leader, *The Times*, 16 June 1884, p. 11.

15 'The Luxuries of the Poor', *The Times*, 5 March 1914, p. 9.

16 Henry Thoreau, journal entry for 24 November 1860, http://thoreau.library.ucsb.edu.

4 Hawaiian Pineapple

1 Kaori O'Connor, 'The Hawaiian *Luau*: Food as Tradition, Transgression, Transformation and Travel', *Food Culture and Society*, XI/2 (2008), pp. 149–72. Sophie Coe Prize, 2009.
2 Gilbert Grosvenor, 'The Hawaiian Islands', *National Geographic Magazine*, LXV, no. 2 (February 1924), p. 168.
3 E. V. Wilcox, 'The Pineapple Industry', *Paradise of the Pacific*, Honolulu (December 1911), p. 42.
4 Hawaiian Pineapple Growers Association advertisement, *Ladies Home Journal* (1 March 1909), p. 66.
5 Hawaiian Pineapple Growers Association advertisement, *Ladies Home Journal* (April 1909), p. 72.
6 Association of Hawaiian Pineapple Canners advertisement, *National Geographic Magazine* (February 1924), p. 250.
7 Dole Company, *A Hawaiian Luau*, n.d. (*c.* 1950s), p. 1.
8 *Del Monte Luau Favourites and Island Recipes*, n.d., p. 1.

5 Drinking the Pineapple

1 Samuel Eliot Morison, *Journals and Other Documents on the Life and Voyages of Christopher Columbus* (New York, 1963), p. 346.
2 Peter Martyr d'Anghiera, *De Orbe Nova: The Eight Decades of Peter Martyr D'Anghiera*, trans. with notes and an introduction by Frances Augustus MacNutt (New York, 1912), vol. I, p. 237.
3 Joyce Lorimer, ed., *Sir Walter Ralegh's 'Discoverie of Guiana'* (London, 2006), p. 206.
4 Richard Ligon, *A True and Exact History of the Island of Barbadoes* [1763] (London, 1970), p. 33.
5 D. P. Bartholomew, Robert E. Paull and K. E. Rohrbach, eds, *The Pineapple: Botany, Production and Uses* (Honolulu, HI, 2002).
6 Hugh Barty-King and Anton Massel, *Rum Yesterday and Today*, with a foreword by Hammond Innes (London, 1983).

7 William Terrington, *Cooling Cups and Dainty Drinks* (London, 1870), p. 52.

8 George Smith, distiller, *The Nature of Fermentation Explain'd* (London, 1729), pp. 16–17.

9 'A Bevy of Women Charged with Drunkenness', *Pall Mall Gazette*, 27 December 1867, issue 898.

10 Richard A. Hawkins, *A Pacific Industry* (London, 2011), p. 87.

11 American Can Company, *The Hawaiian Islands and the Story of Pineapple* (New York, 1939), p. 37.

12 Victor Bergeron, *Trader Vic's Book of Food and Drink* (New York, 1946), p. 60.

13 For original recipe see Victor Bergeron, *Trader Vic's Rum Cookery and Drinkery* (New York, 1974), p. 133.

6 Global Pineapple

1 'Miss Shaw on the Australian Outlook', *The Times*, 10 January 1894, p. 11.

2 Kaori O'Connor, 'The King's Christmas Pudding: Globalization, Recipes and the Commodities of Empire', *Journal of Global History*, 4 (2009), pp. 127–55.

3 Empire Marketing Board, *A Book of Empire Dinners* (London, 1928), p. 51.

4 In J. L. Collins, *The Pineapple: Botany, Cultivation and Utilization* (London, 1960), p. 10.

Select Bibliography

Bartholomew, D. P., with Robert E. Paull and K. G. Rohrbach, eds, *The Pineapple: Botany, Production and Uses* (Wallingford, CT, and New York, 2003)

Beauman, Fran, *The Pineapple: King of Fruits* (London, 2005)

Bergeron, Victor J., *Bartender's Guide* (New York, 1947)

——, *Trader Vic's Rum Cookery and Drinkery* (New York, 1974)

Coe, Sophie, *America's First Cuisines* (Austin, TX, 1994)

Collins, J. L., *The Pineapple: Botany, Cultivation and Utilization* (London, 1960)

Hawkins, Richard A., *A Pacific Industry: A History of Pineapple Canning in Hawaii* (London, 2011)

Johnson, G. W., *The Pineapple: Its Culture, Use and History* (London, 1847)

O'Connor, Kaori, 'The Hawaiian *Luau*: Food as Tradition, Transgression, Transformation and Travel', *Food Culture and Society*, XI/2 (2008), pp. 149–72

Okihiro, Gary, *Pineapple Culture: A History of the Tropical and Temperate Zones* (Berkeley, CA, and London, 2009)

Roche, Thomas W. E., *A Pineapple for the King* (London, 1971)

Websites and Associations

Dole
www.dole.com (USA)

Delmonte
www.delmonte.com (USA)
www.kitchenomics.com (Philippines)

Libby's recipes
www.ilovelibbys.com (USA)

Australia
www.taste.com.au www.goldencircle.com.au

New Zealand
www.dolenz.co.nz

South Africa
www.pineapples.co.za

Mexico
www.yummly.com

Brazil
www.brazilianfruit.org
www.cookbrasil.com

Acknowledgements

This book is dedicated with much love to Paul Sidey, dear friend and brilliant editor and photographer, who read drafts of this book, shot pictures for me in the palaces of Spain and the jungles of Cornwall, and gave me lovely lunches and dinners at which we ate and drank everything but pineapples. Thanks are due to Michael Leaman, and Andy Smith, Harry Gilonis and Martha Jay of Reaktion Books; Juleigh Muirhead Clark of the Colonial Williamsburg Foundation; Stacey Chandler of the John F. Kennedy Presidential Library; and Joan Hori of the University of Hawaii Manoa Library. I am grateful to Gillian Riley and Helen Saberi for warm companionship and many helpful suggestions, Timothy O'Sullivan for buoyant wit and wisdom, Noel and Daloni Rees for endless *hwyl,* Anastasia Berry for *barong Tagalog,* Sarah Byrne for fun fieldwork, Rachel Laudan for 'tablecloth stainer', David Judd for encouragement and patience, Rina Gill for pineapple earrings, Marianne Velmans for happy hospitality over many years, Martha Yamashiro for pineapple spareribs, Thomas Elliott for Pineapple Lumps and my daughter Kira Eva Tokiko Kalihilihiokekaiokanaloa Ffion Lusela Hopkins for being her wonderful self.

Photo Acknowledgements

The author and the publishers wish to express their thanks to the below sources of illustrative material and/or permission to reproduce it.

Photo © adlifemarketing/iStock www.istockphoto.com: p. 102; photo © AlexanderZam/iStock www.istockphoto.com: p. 44; photo © AndrewLam/iStock www.istockphoto.com: p. 126; author's collection: pp. 66, 97; photo © BackyardProduction/iStock www. istockphoto. com: p. 62; The British Museum, London: pp. 9, 10, 13, 14, 26, 34, 37, 43, 45, 57; photos © The Trustees of the British Museum, London: pp. 8, 9, 10, 13, 14, 26, 31, 34, 35, 37, 38, 40, 43, 45, 51, 57, 106, 110; photos © edoneil/iStock www. istockphoto. com: p. 58, 101; photo © evgenyb/iStock www.istockphoto.com: p. 116; photo © fesoj/iStock www.istockphoto.com: p. 50; photo © FourOaks/iStock www.istockphoto.com: p. 128; Ham House, Surrey (Stapleton Collection): p. 23; photo © hofred/iStock www. istockphoto.com: p. 127; photo © imagestock/iStock www. istockphoto.com: p. 93; photo © ivanmateev/iStock www.istock-photo. com: p. 115; photo © janeps/iStock www.istockphoto.com: p. 121; photo © Juanmonino/iStock www.istockphoto.com: p. 100; photo © kcastagnola/iStock www.istockphoto.com: p. 28; photo Lisa Larsen: p. 63; photos Library of Congress, Washington, DC: pp. 59, 64, 90–91; photo © logneticstock/iStock www.istockphoto. com: p. 109; photo © lucato/iStock www.istockphoto.com: p. 108; photo © matka_Wariatka/iStock www.istockphoto.com: p. 123;

Index

italic numbers refer to illustrations; **bold** to recipes